ISLAMIC FINANCE

Basic Concepts and Issues

Hussein Elasrag

Islamic Finance: Basic Concepts and Issues

Hussein Elasrag

Table of Contents

1. Introduction:

Islamic finance is the only example of a financial system directly based on the ethical precepts of a major religion, providing not only investment guidelines but also a set of unique investment and financing products." Islamic finance is based on *Shari'ah*, the Islamic law that provides guidelines for multiple aspects of Muslim life, including religion, politics, economics, banking, business and aspects of the legal system What *Shari'ah* compliant financing (SCF) seeks to do is to shape financial practices and accompanying legal instruments that conform to Islamic law. Major financial principles of Shari'ah include a ban on interest, a ban on uncertainty, adherence to risk-sharing and profit-sharing, promotion of ethical investments that enhance society and do not violate practices banned in the *Qur'an* and tangible asset-backing.(Elasrag, 9. April 2011)

Money, according to Islamic teachings is a measure of value, not a commodity. Debt is a relationship in which risk and responsibility are shared by all parties to a contract.

Money must be put to practical use in creating real value for the participants of the transaction. It must be used to create, and not be a commodity in on and of itself. It because of this that the perception of hoarding capital, and the earning of a passive return on capital keyed to the passage of time, -i.e. interest – is prohibited. In short, money must not be made from money.

The establishment of modern Islamic financial institutions started three decades ago. Currently, there are at least 70 countries that have some form of Islamic financial services; almost all major multinational banks are offering these services. The underlying financial principles in Islamic finance have remained unchanged historically since their development over 1,400 years ago. Financial products must be certified as Sharia compliant by an expert in Islamic law. Certification requires that the transaction adheres to a number of key principles that include:(Chapra, 2011)

- Backing by a tangible asset, usufruct or services, so as to avoid 'speculation' (gharar). Prohibition of interest payments (riba).

- Risk to be shared amongst participants.
- Limitations on sale of financial assets and their use as collateral.
- Prohibition of finance for activities deemed incompatible with sharia law (haram), such as alcohol, conventional financial services, gambling and tobacco.

Modern Islamic finance emerged in the mid-1970s with the founding of the first large Islamic banks. Development initially occurred through marketing of a steadily expanding supply of Sharia compliant financial instruments.

This supply-driven model contributed to relatively slow growth until the mid-1990s, since when demand has increasingly driven the development of Islamic financial instruments. Rising awareness and demand for Islamic products, along with supportive government policies and growing sophistication of financial institutions, have together raised the rate of growth.

Two developments have been critical to the expansion of Islamic financial markets. In 1998, the so-called "Dow

Jones Islamic Indexes *fatwa*" played a transformative role because it opened the door to a limited degree of "permissible impurity" in financial transactions and institutionalized a notion of cleansing and purification whereby small amounts of impermissible interest income could be cleansed or purified by donation to charity. In turn, this led to a series of equity investment tests that could be used to evaluate potential investments for *Shari'ah* compliance. A second critical innovation was the introduction of *sukuk* – a *Shari'ah* compliant substitute for bonds – where capital protection is achieved not as a loan but as a binding agreement by the issuer to repurchase certain assets over a period of time.

Sukuk has now become one of the backbones of Islamic capital markets and has enabled the rapid growth of Islamic financial transactions.

While the Islamic finance industry represents a fraction of the global finance market, it has grown at double-digit rates in recent years. By some estimates, total assets held globally under Islamic finance reached $1 trillion in 2010. Islamic banks have appeared to be more resilient than conventional banks to the immediate effects of the international financial crisis and global economic downturn. Some analysts have attributed this to Islamic banks' avoidance of speculative activities. However, the Islamic finance industry has not been completely immune to the general decline in demand and investor uncertainty.

TheCityUK estimates that the global market for Islamic financial services ,as measured by Sharia compliant assets, reached $1,460bn at the end of 2012, up a fifth on the previous year. This means that global assets of Islamic finance have doubled since the start of the economic slowdown. The industry is set to grow significantly in the years ahead. At the current rate of growth of around 20% per year, the market could top $2 trillion in assets by the end of 2014.(UK Islamic finance secretariat UKIFS, 2013) Assets that can be allocated to individual countries from The Banker's survey reveals that the leading countries for Sharia compliant assets are Iran which accounts for around 36% of the global market, Malaysia (17%) and Saudi Arabia (14%). These are followed by other Gulf states including UAE, Kuwait, Bahrain and Qatar, and then Turkey.The UK, in ninth place, is the leading Western country with $19bn of reported assets.There are over 700 institutions registered globally as sharia-compliant organisations in financial services. Of these, around 500 are fully compliant, and the remainder operate sharia-compliant products within a conventional institution. Countries with most of the 430 firms reporting to The Banker's survey include Bahrain and Indonesia with 74 and 71 firms respectively. Malaysia, Iran, Kuwait and Saudi Arabia were in a group of countries with more than 50 firms.(UK Islamic finance secretariat UKIFS, 2013)

The multiple reasons for the growth of the Islamic financial sector in recent years:(Alasrag, 2010)

(1) The flow of funds into Muslim oil-producing states;

(2) Growing political and social desire in the Muslim world for financial alternatives to banking and investment institutions that have been historically dominated by the West;

(3) The spreading credit crisis in global financial markets

and the need to access new sources of investment capital;

(4) The growth of sovereign wealth funds and the desire to have Shari'ah compliant instruments through which to invest them; and,

(5) The rapidly accelerating number of cross-border multi- jurisdictional financial transactions that are possible and required in a globalized world economy Assets held by Muslim investors worldwide now exceed $1.6 trillion, and that amount is expected to grow to $2.7 trillion by 2010.

Shari'ah compliant finance has become an accepted and vibrant element in international financial transactions. It offers a fresh opportunity to emphasize the moral and ethical aspects of business and finance that reaches beyond the Arab and Islamic worlds to prompt a reexamination of the core values underlying all global financial transactions – making available the financial resources needed to develop the human capital that will sustain economic and social progress. The main principles of Islamic finance include:

(1)The prohibition of taking or receiving interest;

(2)Capital must have a social and ethical purpose beyond pure, unfettered return;

(3)Investments in businesses dealing with alcohol, gambling, drugs or anything else that the Shari'ah considers unlawful are deemed undesirable and prohibited;

(4)A prohibition on transactions involving maysir (speculation or gambling); and

(5)A prohibition on gharar, or uncertainty about the subject- matter and terms of contracts – this includes a prohibition on selling something that one does not own.

Because of the restriction on interest-earning investments, Islamic banks must obtain their earnings through profit-sharing investments or fee-based returns. When loans are given for business purposes, the lender, if he wants to make a legitimate gain under the Shari'ah, should take part in the risk. If a lender does not take part in the risk, his receipt of any gain over the amount loaned is classed as interest. Islamic financial institutions also have the flexibility to engage in leasing transactions, including leasing transactions with purchase options.

It may be asked why non-Muslims would agree to use Islamic finance structures. The principal answer is that Islamic finance provides an opportunity to tap into the significant funds of Islamic investors seeking Shari'ah compliant investments. In addition, Islamic finance can be combined with conventional funding sources and export credit agency (ECA) support.

As the Islamic finance industry develops further, there is a growing need for standardization and professionalism across the industry. Coupled with this is the importance of adopting robust corporate governance systems of internationally recognized standards incorporating transparent, fair and ethical working practices. Islamic financial institutions are well-placed in this context, since at the heart of Islamic law is a vision of social development which requires all individuals and businesses to conduct themselves ethically and in a socially responsible manner.

This Book tries to note the main Principal of Islamic

finance. In addition to discuss the Improvement can be made in several areas to promote and enhance the providing Islamic financial services.

II. Fundamentals of the Islamic finance

One of the most important objectives of Islam is to realize greater justice in human society. According to the Qur'an all the messengers of God were sent to promote justice and any society where there is no justice will ultimately head towards decline and destruction. One of the essential requisites for ensuring justice is a set of rules or moral values, which everyone accepts and complies with faithfully. The financial system may be able to promote justice if, in addition to being strong and stable, it satisfies at least two conditions. One of these is that the financier should also share in the risk so as not to shift the entire burden of losses to the entrepreneur or the borrower, and the other is that an equitable share of the society's financial resources becomes available to even the poor on affordable terms in keeping with their ability to repay so as to enable them to realize their dream of owning their own homes, pursuing higher education and vocational training, and establishing their own micro enterprises.

To fulfill the first condition of justice, Islam requires both the financier and the entrepreneur to equitably share the profit as well as the loss. For this purpose, one of the basic principles of Islamic finance is: "No risk, no gain." This should help introduce greater discipline into the financial system by motivating financial institutions to assess the risks more carefully and to effectively monitor the use of funds by borrowers. The double assessment of risks by both the financier and the entrepreneur should help inject greater discipline into the system, and go a long way in not only increasing efficiency in the use of resources but also reducing excessive lending.(Chapra, 2011)

Islamic finance is based on Shari'ah, an Arabic term that is often translated into "Islamic law". Shari'ah provides guidelines for aspects of Muslim life, including religion, politics, economics, banking, business, and law. Shari'ah-compliant financing (SCF) constitutes financial practices that conform to Islamic law.(Ilias, 2010)

Islamic finance was practiced predominantly in the Muslim world throughout the Middle Ages, fostering trade and business activities with the development of credit. In Spain and the Mediterranean and Baltic states, Islamic merchants became indispensable middlemen for trading activities. In fact, many concepts, techniques, and instruments of Islamic finance were later adopted by European financiers and businessmen.

In contrast, the term "Islamic financial system" is relatively new, appearing only in the mid-1980s. In fact, all the earlier references to commercial or mercantile activities conforming to Islamic principles were made under the umbrella of either "interest free" or "Islamic" banking. However, describing the Islamic financial system simply as "interest-free" does not provide a true picture of the system as a whole. Undoubtedly, prohibiting the receipt and payment of interest is the nucleus of the system, but it is supported by other principles of Islamic doctrine advocating risk sharing, individuals' rights and duties, property rights, and the sanctity of contracts.

Similarly, the Islamic financial system is not limited to banking but covers capital formation, capital markets, and all types of financial intermediation. Interpreting the system as "interest free" tends to create confusion. The philosophical foundation of an Islamic financial system goes beyond the interaction of factors of production and economic behavior. Whereas the conventional financial system focuses primarily on the economic and financial aspects of transactions, the Islamic system places equal emphasis on the ethical, moral, social, and religious dimensions, to enhance equality and fairness for the good of society as a whole. The system can be fully appreciated only in the context of Islam's teachings on the work ethic, wealth distribution, social and economic justice, and the role of the state.

The Islamic financial system is founded on the absolute prohibition of the payment or receipt of any predetermined, guaranteed rate of return. This closes the door to the concept of interest and precludes the use of debt-based instruments. The system encourages risk-sharing, promotes entrepreneurship, discourages speculative behavior, and emphasizes the sanctity of contracts. Modern Islamic finance has existed internationally since the 1970s. Currently, Islamic finance represents a small but growing segment of the global finance industry.

In recent years, SCF has expanded to other parts of the world. Islamic finance is growing in Europe and North America, areas in which Muslims are in the minority. In August 2004, the United Kingdom's Financial Services Authority (FSA) approved a banking license for the Islamic Bank of Britain (IBB), the country's first Islamic bank. The IBB would serve the consumer market with *Shari'ah*-compliant products. In March 2006, the FSA licensed the European Islamic Investment Bank as the United Kingdom's first independent bank for *Shari'ah*-compliant investments. In 1999, the Dow Jones presented its first Islamic market index, which follows *Shari'ah*-compliant stocks internationally. The Dow Jones maintains more than 70 indices in its Islamic series and is advised by an independent *Shari'ah* Supervisory Board counsel.[1]

In 2006, S&P Dow Jones Indices introduced the S&P Shari'ah Indices. Recognizing the urgent need for indices, which are a real gauge of the global equity markets and well-established standards, S&P Dow Jones Indices initially applied Shari'ah screens to three headline indices – the S&P 500, the S&P Europe 350 and the S&P Japan 500. The results are the S&P 500 Shari'ah, the S&P Europe 350 Shari'ah and the S&P Japan 500 Shari'ah indices. In 2007, S&P Dow Jones Indices followed with the S&P

[1] The Dow Jones Islamic Market Index (DJIM), launched in 1999 in Bahrain, was the first index created for investors seeking investments in compliance with Muslim Sharia law.The DJIM has an independent Shari'ah (islamic Law) Supervisory Board. The DJIM screens have been adopted by the Accounting and Auditing Organization for Islamic Financial Institutions ("AAOIFI")-Standard 21. The DJIM measure the performance of a global universe of investable equities that have been screened for Shari'ah compliance consistent with Dow Jones Indexes' methodology. The selection universe for the DJIM family of indexes is the same as the universe for the Dow Jones World Index, a broad-market index that seeks to provide approximately 95% market coverage of 44 countries. The first level of DJIM screening removes companies involved in such products alcohol, pork-related products, conventional financial services (e.g. banks and insurance companies), entertainment (e.g. hotels, casinos, gambling etc.), tobacco, and weapons and defense. A second level of DJIM screening based on financial ratios, is intended to remove companies based on debt and interest income levels in their balance sheets. Stocks of companies that pass both sets of screens are included in the DJIM. All other indexes in the DJIM family are created as subsets of this benchmark. See: http://en.wikipedia.org/wiki/Dow_Jones_Islamic_Market_Index

GCC Shari'ah and the S&P Pan Asia Shari'ah Indices, to cater to the demand for a benchmark Shari'ah product for those regions. Currently, S&P Dow Jones Indices boasts the most comprehensive series of Shari'ah indices in the industry. This was accomplished in 2008 with the completion of the review of the S&P Global BMI Index, which consists of over 10,000 companies worldwide, for Shari'ah compliance. The result is the S&P Global BMI Shari'ah index, comprised of nearly 4,000 constituents, along with 10 sector and 45 country and regional sub-indices. These are gauges of major markets, sectors, and regions; and by screening out stocks that are not Shari'ah compliant, they become ideal investment vehicles for observant Muslims.(S&P Dow Jones Indices, March 2014, p. 3)

A. ***Shari'ah* law defined**

Shari'ah(or Islamic) law is meant to regulate all aspects of a Muslim's way of life. It is broadly divided into two sets of rules: one relates to the obligatory worship of God (*ibadah*) and the other relates to daily life outside the context of obligatory worship (*muamalat*), including commercial and financial dealings. *Shari'ah* is not a codified body of law. It consists of general rules and principles derived from the *Qur'an* (the Muslim holy book), the practices (*sunnah*) and sayings (*ahadith*) of the Prophet Mohammed (as discussed in further detail below). These general principles are capable of interpretation and development to address new issues or circumstances that arise from time to time. Indeed, the *Shari'ah* has been supplemented by extensive Islamic jurisprudence (*fiqh*) developed over centuries by different schools of thought (the *madhaa'hib*). The key point to note is that, while all the schools of thought agree on the fundamental *Shari'ah* principles enshrined in the *Qur'an*, *sunnah* and *hadith*, they sometimes hold differing views on their interpretation and application.

B. Sources of *Shari'ah* law

*Shari'ah*l aw is derived from a number of primary and secondary sources.(Allen&OveryLLP, 2009)

1. Qur'an

The *Qur'an* is a primary source of law and is believed by Muslims to contain the word of God as revealed to the Prophet Mohammed. Evidence found in other sources of *Shari'ah* law is subject to the *Qur'an.*

2. Sunnah

Sunnah literally means "well known path". The *Sunnah* is a primary source of law and comprises traditional accounts of what the Prophet Mohammed said or did during his life

Which have legal content. *Sunnah* also comprises the sayings of others tacitly approved by the Prophet's silence.

3. Hadith

A further primary source of law is the narrative record of sayings and actions of the Prophet Mohammed known as *hadith* (plural *ahadith*). The extent to which *sunnah* is derived or differentiated from *ahadith* depends on the context and school of thought being considered.

4. Qiyas

Qiyas represents the process of reasoning whereby the principles found in the *Qur'an* and *sunnah* are extended to new cases by analogy.

5. Ijma

Ijma represents the consensus of the Islamic community (whether at a local or global academic level) on a particular issue.

6. Ijtihad

Ijtihad is the interpretation and the opinion of Islamic jurists on a particular issue. *Qiyas*,*ijma* and *ijtihad* are all secondary sources of *Shari'ah* law.

C. Issues relating to interpretation and application of Shari'ah law

Since *Shari'ah* law is not a single codified body of law and is open to interpretation, the opinions of *Shari'ah* scholars may differ on the same question of *Shari'ah* law depending on the school of thought to which particular scholars belong. In addition, scholars' views on questions of *Shari'ah* law may change over time. This can lead to uncertainty and inconsistency of interpretation and application of *Shari'ah* law across the Islamic world.(Allen&OveryLLP, 2009; Ayub, 2009)

1. Key Shari'ah principles and prohibitions relevant to finance

There are a number of key *Shari'ah* principles and prohibitions relevant to finance and commercial transactions which distinguish Islamic finance from the conventional forms. For completeness, it should be mentioned that there are two main branches within Islam: *sunnism* and *shiaism*. The majority of Muslims are *sunni* and the following is limited to the discussion of the general *Shari'ah* principles relating to Islamic finance within *sunni* jurisprudence. The key *Shari'ah* principles which underpin Islamic finance, and have led to the creation of a separate finance industry, are as follows:(Allen&OveryLLP, 2009)

a) *Prohibition on usury and interest (riba)*

Prohibition of interest. Prohibition of *riba*, a term literally meaning "an excess" and interpreted as "any unjustifiable increase of capital whether in loans or sales" is the central tenet of the system. More precisely, any positive, fixed, predetermined rate tied to the maturity and the amount of principal (i.e., guaranteed regardless of the performance of the investment) is considered *riba* and is prohibited. The general consensus among Islamic scholars is that *riba* covers not only Usury but also the charging of "interest" as widely practiced. This prohibition is based on arguments of social justice, equality, and property rights. Islam encourages the earning of profits but forbids the charging of interest because profits, determined ex post, symbolize successful entrepreneurship and creation of additional wealth whereas interest, determined ex ante, is a cost that is accrued irrespective of the outcome of business operations and may not create wealth if there are business losses. Social justice demands that borrowers and lenders share rewards as well as losses in an equitable fashion and that the process of wealth accumulation and distribution in the economy be fair and representative of true productivity.

Under the *Shari'ah*, it is not permissible to charge, pay or receive interest. The *Shari'ah* does not recognize the time value of money and it is therefore not permissible to make money by lending it. Money must be used to create real economic value and it is only permissible to earn a return from investing money in permissible commercial activities which involve the financier or investor taking some commercial risk. This prohibition is the main driving force behind the development of the modern Islamic finance industry. *Riba* can take one of two forms: *riba al- naseeyah* and *riba al-fadl.*(Dewar & Hussain, 2011, p. 274)

1- Riba al-naseeyah is the amount of excess received by a lender in addition to the capital amount lent. This type of *riba* is comparable to the traditional concept of interest in conventional lending activities.

2- The second type, *riba al-fadl,* is excess compensation

without any form of consideration in return.

In modern finance, *riba al-fadl* could be applicable to several exchange of commodities contracts.

The idea is that when compensation is paid, it should be justified or be set against a specific activity and the return should also be associated with a specific risk. Therefore when parties exchange commodities of similar value and one party pays excessive compensation to the other party, this is

Considered *riba.*

b) Prohibition on realising a gain from speculation (mayseer)

It is not permissible to earn a profit from speculation. Gambling is therefore not permitted under *Shari'ah.* Any contracts or arrangements which involve speculation are also not permitted. That said, it is accepted under the *Shari'ah* that there is an element of speculation in most commercial arrangements and, unlike the absolute prohibition of interest, it is a question of the degree of speculation involved and whether the intention behind the transaction is to realise a gain from some productive effort or purely speculation.

The distinction between prohibited speculation and legitimate commercial speculation is not always clear in practice and there are examples where it can be difficult to distinguish between the two. For example, it is generally accepted that it is permissible to make an equity investment in a company Engaging in a business activity that is permissible under the *Shari'ah* with a view to realising future dividends and capital gains on the investment. There is of course a degree of commercial speculation involved about the future prospects of the company when an investor makes an equity investment, but whether such speculation is permissible or not would depend on the intention of the investor, i.e. was the intention to make a quick profit by speculating in the likely movement of the share price over a very short period of time (as is arguably the case with day trading), or was the decision made on the basis of careful evaluation of the company's past results and future prospects?At the other end of the spectrum, equity derivatives such as index-linked derivatives are generally viewed as unacceptable under *Shari'ah* because they involve speculation on the movement of an equity index.(Allen&OveryLLP, 2009)

c) No uncertainty (gharar) in commercial transactions

Certainty of terms in any transaction is a key requirement under the *Shari'ah*. Again, as with speculation, a degree of commercial uncertainty is acceptable but there must not be any uncertainty about the key terms of the transaction. For example, in a transaction for the sale of assets, the sale contract should set out a clear description of the assets being sold, the sale price and the time for delivering the assets to the purchaser. Similarly, a leasing contract needs to set out clearly the assets which are being leased, the duration of the lease and the rent payable under the lease. One of the reasons that conventional insurance contracts are not considered permissible under the *Shari'ah* is that there is no certainty as to when a claim will be paid, given that there is no way of knowing if and when the insured event will occur. In the context of modern day Islamic finance, key examples of *gharar* are:(Allen&OveryLLP, 2009; Uusmani, 2002)

(a) Advising a customer to buy shares of a particular company that is the subject of a takeover bid, on the grounds that its share price can be expected to rise;

(b) Buying a house, the price of which is to be specified in the future;

(c) When the subject matter or specifications to a contract are unknown; and

(d) Deferred payment under a contract where the deferment is for an unknown period.

d) All activity must be for permitted purposes (halal)

Muslims must not engage in (or derive any benefit from) activities which are prohibited under the *Shari'ah*. It is therefore not permissible for Muslims to invest in businesses which engage in prohibited activities such as casinos, a breweries or a factories making pork products. It is also not permissible for Islamic banks to provide any financing to such businesses. However, a very strict interpretation of these rules would mean that Muslims would only be able to invest in a very limited number of businesses internationally. For example, it would not be permissible for Muslims to invest in a hotel that serve alcohol, a food company which also manufactures pork products as part of its product range or any business that lends or borrows money at interest.

In light of the practical considerations of international commerce and in order to enable Muslim investors to participate in it, a number of prominent *Shari'ah* scholars have advanced the view that it is permissible for Muslims to invest in businesses or companies which are not entirely *Shari'ah* compliant so long as certain conditions are met. These conditions include (among other things):

(a) The principal business activity must be permissible under *Shari'ah*;

(b) Any income derived from prohibited activities should only form a small percentage of the overall income of the company or business (this percentage ranges from 5 to 20 per cent. Of overall income depending upon the nature of the prohibited activity and the *Shari'ah* scholars involved);

(c) The aggregate amount of interest-bearing debt incurred by a company or business must not exceed a certain percentage of

its assets or market capitalization (there are disagreements between *Shari'ah* scholars as to what percentage is acceptable and it ranges from 25 to 35 per cent. of total assets or market capitalization depending upon the scholars involved); and

(d) The accounts receivable of the company on the business must not exceed a certain percentage of its assets or market capitalization (usually set between 25 and 33 per cent.).

e) Making Money from Money is not Permissible

One of the wrong presumptions on which all theories of interest are based is that money is a commodity. It is, therefore, argued that just as a merchant can sell his commodity for a higher price than his cost, he can also sell his money for a higher price than its face value, or just as he can lease his property and can charge a rent against it, he can also lend his money and can claim interest thereupon. Islamic principles, however, do not subscribe to this presumption. Money and commodity have different characteristics and, therefore, they are treated differently.

The basic points of difference between money and commodity:-

(a) Money has no intrinsic utility. It cannot be utilized in direct fulfillment of human needs. It can only be used for acquiring some goods or services. A commodity, on the other hand, has intrinsic utility and can be utilized directly without exchanging it for some other thing.

(b) Commodities can be of different qualities while money has no quality except that it is a measure of value or a medium of exchange. Therefore, all the units of money of the same denomination, are hundred per cent equal to each other. An old and dirty note of SR.100 has the same value as a brand new note of SR.100.

(c) In commodities, the transactions of sale and purchase are effected on an identified particular commodity. If A has purchased a particular car by pinpointing it, and seller has agreed, he deserves to receive the same car. The seller cannot compel him to take the delivery of another car, though of the same type or quality. Money, on the contrary, cannot be pinpointed in a transaction of exchange. If A has purchased a commodity from B by showing him a particular note of 100 SR.100 he can still pay him another note of the same denomination.

Based on these basic differences, Islamic *Shari'ah* has treated money differently from commodities, especially on two scores: Firstly, money (of the same denomination) is not held to be the subject matter of trade, like other commodities. Its use has been restricted to its basic purpose i.e. to act as a medium of exchange and a measure of value. Secondly, if for exceptional reasons, money has to be exchanged for money or it is borrowed, the payment on both sides must be equal, so that it is not used for the purpose it is not meant for i.e. trade in money itself. In short, money is treated as "potential" capital. It becomes actual capital only when it joins hands with other resources to undertake a productive activity. Islam recognizes the time value of money, but only when it acts as capital, not when it is "potential" capital.

2. Regulation of Islamic Finance

Financial institutions seeking to offer Shari'ah-compliant products typically have a Shari'ah supervisory board (or at a minimum, a Shari'ah counselor). The Shari'ah board is to review and approve financial practices and activities for compliance with Islamic principles. Such expertise raises the attractiveness of Shari'ah- compliant financial intermediaries to investors considering Islamic banking. International institutions have been established to promote international consistency in Islamic finance. The Accounting and Auditing Organization for Islamic Financial Institutions (AAOIFI), founded in 1991 and located in Bahrain, issues international standards on accounting, auditing, and corporate governance. It has 200 members from 45 countries; its membership includes central banks, Islamic financial institutions, and other bodies in the Islamic banking and finance industry. Another regulatory body is the Islamic Financial Services Boards (IFSB), which began operations in 2003 and is based in Malaysia. IFSB puts forth standards for supervision and regulation. Many leading Islamic financial centers around the world have adopted international SCF regulation standards.U.S. federal banking regulators have provided some formal guidance about Islamic products. The Office of the Comptroller of the Currency (OCC) issued two directives concerning Shari'ah compliant mortgage products. In 1997, the OCC issued guidance about *ijara* ("lease"), a financial structure in which the financial intermediary purchases and subsequently leases an asset to a consumer for a fee. In 1999, the OCC recognized *murabaha* ("cost-plus"), under which the financial intermediary buys an asset for a customer with the understanding that the customer will buy the asset back for a higher fee.

Standardization of Islamic finance regulations has been of increasing interest in the industry. Shari'ahis open to interpretation and Islamic scholars are not in complete agreement regarding what constitutes SCF. Islamic finance laws and regulatory practices vary across countries. The lack of concurrent viewpoints makes it difficult to standardize Islamic financing.

Standardization also may be challenging because the maturity of Islamic finance markets varies from country to country, with some markets well-established and others that are more nascent. Without standardization, some industry officials express concern that Shari'ah-compliance risk may grow. The lack of standardization across Islamic finance markets raises legal uncertainty that a contract will not be recognized as valid under Islamic law by all Islamic scholars. This uncertainty has been highlighted by a recent dispute between Lebanon's Blom Bank and Kuwait's Islamic firm Investment Dar over whether or not a contract between the two entities was compliant with Islamic principles and if payment should be made. Many observers view standardization of SCF regulations as important in increasing the marketability and acceptance of Islamic products. Over the years, there have been numerous initiatives to improve regulatory practices. For example, in 2009, the IFSB published guiding principals on issues such as governance and capital adequacy requirements for various financial products. The AAOIFI is in the process of developing new standards in risk management and corporate governance.

1. Basic Islamic financial instruments

Islamic markets offer different instruments to satisfy providers and users of funds in a variety of ways: sales, trade financing, and investment. Basic instruments include cost-plus financing (*murabaha*), profit-sharing (*mudaraba*) ,leasing (*ijara*), partnership (*musharaka*) ,and for ward sale (*bay' salam*), Deferred-payment sale (*bay' mu'ajjal*) and deferred-delivery sale (*bay'salam*) contracts, in addition to spot sales, are used for conducting credit sales. In a deferred-payment sale, delivery of the product is taken on the spot but delivery of the payment is delayed for an agreed period. Payment can be made in a lump sum or in installments, provided there is no extra charge for the delay. A deferred-delivery sale is similar to a forward contract where delivery of the product is in the future in exchange for payment on the spot market.(Iqbal, 1997) These instruments serve as the basic building blocks for developing a wide array of more complex financial instruments, suggesting that there is great potential for financial innovation and expansion in Islamic financial markets.

There are several methods of Islamic financing. However, in the world of commercial financing and more particularly, project financing, certain methods are more commonly encountered than others. These are set out below.

A. **Trade with markup or cost-plus sale (murabaha).** One of the most widely used instruments for short-term financing is based on the traditional notion of purchase finance. The investor undertakes to supply specific goods or commodities, incorporating a mutually agreed contract for resale to the client and a mutually negotiated margin.

Around 75 percent of Islamic financial transactions are cost-plus sales.

Murabaha was originally an exchange transaction in which a trader purchases items required by an end user. The trader then sells those items to the end-user at a price that is calculated using an agreed profit margin over the costs incurred by the trader.

To be in consonance with the principles of Islamic finance governing exchange transactions every *murabaha* transaction must meet the following conditions:

Murabaha transactions may be undertaken only where the client of a bank, or financial institution, wants to purchase a commodity. This type of transaction cannot be effected in cases where the client wants to get funds for a purpose other than purchasing a commodity, like payment of salaries, settlement of bills or other liabilities.

To make it a valid transaction it is necessary that the commodity is really purchased by the bank and it comes into the ownership and possession (physical or constructive) of the bank so that it may assume the risk of the commodity so far as it remains under its ownership and possession.

After acquiring the ownership and possession of the

commodity it should be sold to the client through a valid sale.

Some quarters have equated *murabahah* transactions to interest-based loans. However, there are many significant factors that distinguish a *murabaha* contract from a riba-based one. Some of them are the following:

In the event of default by the end user, the financer only has recourse to the items financed, and no further mark-up or penalty may be applied to the sum outstanding. This means that the amount to be repaid does not go on increasing with passage of time as in the case of amounts borrowed from conventional banks on interest. Also, in conventional financing, the bank gives loans to its clients without ever being concerned how the money is being put to use.

In the event of a *murabahah* transaction, no money is loaned to the client. Rather, the financing party purchases the goods himself, based on the requirement of the client. This ensures that financing is always asset-based. In effect, this type of financing creates real assets and inventories.Another major difference between a *murabahah* contract and an interest-based one is that the financier cannot be unconcerned about the purposes for which the asset being leased is to be put to use. Conventional banks have no compunction in lending to gambling houses or liquor companies, or even pornographic filmmakers.Islamic principles of finance are based on a well-established rule which dictates that "The benefit of a thing is a return for the liability for loss from that thing". Hence, in a *murabahah* transaction the bank or financier assumes the risk by purchasing the commodity before he sells it at a markup. This mark up is considered as the reward of the risk he assumes. Interest-bearing loans assume no risks whatsoever. In other words, because the bank takes title to the goods, and is therefore engaged in buying and selling, its profit derives from a real service that entails a certain risk. This aspect lends the transaction legitimacy.

Most scholars have ruled that, to serve as a deterrent to such as may willfully delay payments, the financer may get the buyer to agree, at the time of the contract, to make a pre-specified donation to an agreed charity in case of late payment of monthly installments.

These scholars, however, caution that this device should be used to the minimum extent and only in cases where *musharakah* or *mudarabah* are not practicable for one reason or another.

B. Profit-sharing agreement (mudaraba).

This is identical to an investment fund in which managers handle a pool of funds. The agent-manager has relatively limited liability while having sufficient incentives to perform. The capital is invested in broadly defined activities, and the terms of profit and risk sharing are customized for each investment. The maturity structure ranges from short to medium term and is more suitable for trade activities.

Mudaraba implies a contract between two parties whereby one party, the *rabb al-mal* (beneficial owner or the sleeping partner), entrusts money to the other party called the *mudarib* (managing trustee or the labour partner). The *mudarib* is to utilize it in an agreed manner and then returns to the rabb al-mal the principal and the pre-agreed share of the profit. He keeps for himself what remains of such profits.

The following rules must govern all *Mudaraba* transactions.(AHMAD, A., & KHAN, M. T. A.1998)

- The division of profits between the two parties must necessarily be on a proportional basis and cannot be a lump sum or guaranteed return.
- The investor is not liable for losses beyond the capital he has contributed. The *mudarib* does not share in the losses except for the loss of his time and efforts.
- Briefly, an Islamic bank lends money to a client to finance a factory, for example, in return for which the bank will get a specified percentage of the factory's net profits every year for a designated period. This share of the profits provides for repayment of the principal and a profit for the bank to pass on to its depositors. Should the factory lose money, the bank, its depositors and the borrower all jointly absorb the losses, thereby putting into practice the pivotal Islamic principle that the providers and users of capital should share risks

and rewards.

Islamic banks use this instrument to finance those seeking investments to run their own enterprises or professional units, whether they be physicians or engineers or traders or craftsmen. The bank provides the adequate finance as a capital owner in exchange of a share in the profit to be agreed upon.

It is worth noting that this mode is a high risk for the bank because the bank delivers capital to the *mudarib* who undertakes the work and management and the *mudarib* shall only be a guarantor in case of negligence and trespass. Islamic banks usually take the necessary precautions to decrease the risk and to guarantee a better execution for the *mudaraba* and pursue this objective with seriousness.

However, it may be noted that, under *mudarabah*, the liability of the financier is limited to the extent of his contribution to the capital, and no more.

C. **Equity participation (musharaka).** This is analogous to a classical joint venture. Both entrepreneur and investor contribute to the capital (assets, technical and managerial expertise, working capital,

etc.) of the operation in varying degrees and agree to share the returns (as well as the risks) in proportions agreed to in advance. Traditionally,this form of transaction has been used for financing fixed assets and working capital of medium- and long-term duration.

Musharaka is a partnership, normally of limited duration, formed to carry out a specific project.

It is, therefore, similar to a Western-style joint venture, and is also regarded by some as the purest form of Islamic financial instrument, since it conforms to the underlying partnership principles of sharing in, and benefiting from, risk. Participation in a *musharaka* can either be in a new project, or by providing additional funds for an existing one. Profits are divided on a pre-determined basis, and any losses shared in proportion to the capital contribution. In this case, the bank enters into a partnership with a client in which both share the equity capital- and maybe even the management -of a project or deal, and both share in the profits or losses according to their equity shareholding. There are two basic types of *musharaka*:(Usmani & Zubairi, 2002)

i. *Sharikah al milk*: partnership based on joint ownership. This may be voluntary e.g. in the purchase of a ship, or involuntary

e.g. as a result of inheritance.

ii. *Sharikah al uqud*: partnership based on a contractual relationship.

There are five subdivisions:

1. *Sharikat al Mufawadah* (full authority and obligation): a limited partnership with equal capital contributions, responsibility, full authority on behalf of others, and responsibility for liabilities,incurred through the normal course of business.

2. *Sharikat al Inan* (restricted authority and obligation): a limited partnership with unequal capital contributions. They do not share equal responsibility, and this reflects their share of the profits.

3. *Sharikat al Wujuh* (goodwill /credit worthiness): companies based on the reputation of one or both

parties, typically small scale business.

4. *Sharikat al Abdan* (labour, skill and management): a company based on the contribution of human efforts, no capital contributions, again, typically small scale business.

5. *Sharikat al Mudaraba*: a *mudaraba*

D. Leasing (ijara). Another popular instrument, accounting for about 10 percent of Islamic financial transactions, is leasing. Leasing is designed for financing vehicles, machinery, equipment, and aircraft.

Different forms of leasing are permissible, including leases where a

portion of the installment payment goes toward the final purchase (with the transfer of ownership to the lessee).

Ijarah can be defined as a process by which " usufruct of a particular property is transferred to another person in exchange for a rent claimed from him/her". In many respects, *Ijarah* resembles leasing as it is practiced in today's commercial world. The distinguishing feature of this mode is that the assets remain the property of the Islamic bank to put them up for rent every time the lease period terminates so as not to remain unutilized for long periods of time. Under *ijarah* the bank or the leasing company assumes the risk of recession or diminishing demand for these assets.

To be in consonance with the principles of Islamic finance governing financial transactions every *ijarah* transaction must meet the following conditions.(Ghuddah, 1998; Usmani & Zubairi, 2002)

- It is a condition that the object leased must not be perishable or consumable.
- The lease is for the utilization not the consumption of the asset.
- It is a condition that the subject of the contract must actually and legally be attainable. It is not permissible to lease something that cannot be delivered.
- The lessee must ensure that the asset is used for

the purpose it is made for. The lessee shall comply with the provisions of the contract. The lessee also shall not benefit from the asset in a way more than what has been agreed upon.

- It is not permitted to lease real estate to be used as an interest based bank or a bar. However it is permissible to lease property to those whose major activities are permissible or *halal* even if they include some secondary prohibited practices.

- The lessor must not only deliver the asset on time, on the date of commencement of lease, but also ensure that the lessor delivers those accessories as well which are essential for the lessee to benefit from the asset as per the norms.
- The lease contract must state the lease period clearly. Renewal terms must also be stated clearly, and things like the rentals for all subsequent years, after the first year, should not mention clauses like 'left to the sole discretion of the lessor' and the like.
- The rental must be money. The lease rent falls due from the receipt of the asset by the lessee, not the

date the contract is signed.

- The amount and timing of the lease payments should be agreed in advance. However, the agreed schedule and amount of those payments need not be uniform.
- It is permissible for the two parties to agree during the lease period to review the lease period or the rental or both. That is because the lease contract occurs periodically unlike the sale contract where the transfer of ownership is immediate.
- The lessor bears the liabilities when leasing the asset such as damage to the asset, payment of premium cost and basic maintenance.
- There is no objection to authorizing the lessee to undertake all the above but the costs thereof must be borne by the lessor/owner.
- The lessor/owner bears all the costs of the legally binding basic maintenance and these are operations on which the permanence and suitability of the leased object depend.

The lessor also bears the cost of the

replacement of durable parts. However, it is permissible to make the lessee bear the cost of ordinary routine maintenance, because this cost is normally known and can be considered as part of the rental.

- The conditions of usage of the leased items must be stated. The lessor must have full possession and legal ownership of the asset prior to leasing it.
- A price cannot be pre-determined for the sale of the asset at the expiry of the lease. However, lessor and lessee may agree to the continuation of the lease or the sale of the leased asset to the lessee under a new agreement at the end of the initial lease period.
- In the event of late payment of rental, the *Ijarah* may be terminated immediately.
- The lessor may claim compensation for any damage caused to the leased assets as a result of negligence on the part of the lessee.

Literally, *Ijarah* means to give something on rent. As a term of Islamic Fiqh, *Ijarah* can also refer to wages paid to a person in consideration of the services rendered by him/her. In the above discussion, the term *Ijarah* is used to represent the usufructs of assets and properties, and not to the services of human beings.

E. **Salam** is one of the basic conditions for the validity of sale in *Shari'ah* that the commodity intended to be sold must be in the physical or constructive possession of the seller. This condition has three implications:

First, the commodity must be existing; a commodity that does not exist at the time of sale cannot be sold.

Second, the seller should have acquired the ownership of that commodity. If the commodity exists but the seller does not own it, he cannot sell it to anybody.

Third, mere ownership is not enough. It should have come in the possession of the seller, either physically or constructively. If the seller owns a commodity, but he has not acquired its delivery by himself or through an agent, he cannot sell it.

There are only two exceptions to this general principle in *shari'a*

. One is *Salam* and the other is *Istisna.* Both are sales of a special nature.

Salam, or *Bay-Salaam* as it is also called, is a sale whereby the seller undertakes to supply some specific goods to the buyer at a future date in exchange for an advanced price fully paid on the spot.

Here the price is paid in cash, but the supply of the purchased goods is deferred. The buyer is called "*Rabb-us-Salam*", the seller is "*Muslam ilaih*", the cash price is "*ra's-ul-mal*", and the purchased commodity is termed as "*muslam fih*".

The *Shari'ah* allows *Salam* subject to certain conditions. The basic purpose of this sale was to meet the needs of the small farmers who needed money to grow their crops and to feed their family up to the time of their harvest. After the prohibition of *riba* they could not take usurious loans. Therefore, it was allowed for them to sell the agricultural products in advance.

Similarly, the traders of Arabia used to export goods to other places and to import other goods to their homeland. They needed money to undertake this type of business. They could not borrow from the usurers after the prohibition of *riba*. It was, therefore, allowed for them that they sell the goods in advance. After receiving their cash price, they could easily undertake the aforesaid business. *Salam* was beneficial to the seller, because he received the price in advance, and it was beneficial to the buyer also, because normally, the price in *Salam* used to be lower than price in spot sales.

The permissibility of *Salam* was an exception to the general rule that prohibits forward sales. Therefore, it was subjected to some strict conditions.

Conditions of *Salam*:[1] (Muhammada & Chonga, 2007; Usmani & Zubairi, 2002, pp. 127-128)

It is necessary for the validity of *Salam* that the buyer pays

[1]Mufti Taqi Usmani ,Forward Sales and Manufacturing Contracts: Salam And Istisna. Available at: http://www.albalagh.net/Islamic_economics/salam_istisna.shtml

the price in full to the seller at the time of effecting the sale. This is necessary because in the absence of full payment by the buyer, it will be tantamount to a sale of debt against debt, which is expressly prohibited. Moreover, the basic wisdom behind the permissibility of *Salam* is to fulfill the instant needs of the seller. If the price is not paid to him in full, the basic purpose of the transaction will be defeated.

Salam can be effected in those commodities only whose quality and quantity can be specified exactly. The things whose quality or quantity is not determined by the specification cannot be sold through the contract of *Salam*. For example, the precious stones cannot be sold on the basis of *Salam*, because every piece of precious stones is normally different from the other either in its quality or in its size or weight and their exact specification is not generally possible.

Salam cannot be effected on a particular commodity or on a product of a particular field or farm.

For example, if the seller undertakes to supply wheat of a particular field, or the fruit of a particular tree, the

Salam will not be valid, because there is a possibility that produce of that particular field or the fruit of that tree is destroyed before the delivery, and in the presence of this possibility the delivery remains uncertain. The same rule is applicable to every commodity whose supply is not certain. It is necessary that the quality of the commodity (intended to be purchased through *Salam*) be fully specified leaving no ambiguity that may lead to dispute. All the possible details in this respect must be expressly mentioned.

It is also necessary that the quantity of the commodity be agreed upon in unequivocal terms. If the commodity is quantified in weights according to the usage of its traders, its weight must be determined, and if it is quantified through measures, its exact measure should be known. What is normally weighed cannot be specified in measures and vice versa.

The exact date of delivery must be specified in the contract. *Salam* cannot be effected in respect of those things that must be delivered at the spot. For example, if gold is purchased in exchange for silver, it is necessary, according to *Shari'ah*, that the delivery of both be simultaneous. Here, *Salam* cannot work. Similarly, if wheat is bartered for barley, the simultaneous delivery of both is necessary for the validity of sale, therefore, the contract of *Salam* in this case is not allowed.

It is permissible to draw a *Salam* sale contract on one whole thing but to be possessed at different times in specific parts.

Salam sale is not permissible on existing commodities because damage and deterioration cannot be assured before delivery on the due date. Delivery may become impossible.

Salam is permissible on a commodity of a specific locality if it is assured that it is almost always available in that locality and it rarely becomes unavailable.

The place of delivery must be stated in the contract if the commodity needs loading or transportation expenses.It is permissible to take mortgage and guarantor on Salam debt to guarantee that the seller satisfies his obligation by delivering the commodity sold, which is a liability on the due date.

It is not permissible for the buyer of a *Salam* commodity to sell it before receiving it because that is similar to the prohibited sale of debts before holding. It is known that the *Salam* commodity is a liability debt on the seller and not an existing commodity. Instead of that, it is permissible for the buyer to draw a parallel *Salam* contract without connecting it to the first Salam contract. *Salam* sale is suitable for the finance of agriculture operations, where the bank can transact with farmers who are expected to have the commodity in plenty during harvest either from their own crops or crops of others, which they can buy and deliver in case their crops fail. Thus the bank renders great services to the farmers in their way to achieve their production targets.

Salam sale is also used to finance commercial and industrial activities, especially phases prior to production and export of commodities and that is by purchasing them on Salam and marketing them for lucrative prices.

The *Salam* sale is applied by banks in financing craftsmen and small producers by supplying them with inputs of production as a *Salam* capital in exchange for some of their commodities to remarket.

The scope of *Salam* sale is large enough to cover the needs of various people such as farmers, industrialists, contractors or traders. It can cover the finance of operational costs and capital goods.

F. **Istisna** is the second kind of sale where a commodity is transacted before it comes into existence.

It means to order a manufacturer to manufacture a specific commodity for the purchaser. If the manufacturer undertakes to manufacture the goods for him, the transaction of *Istisna* comes into

existence. But it is necessary for the validity of *Istisna* that the price is fixed with the consent of the parties and that necessary specification of the commodity (intended to be manufactured) is fully settled between them.

The contract of *Istisna* creates a moral obligation on the manufacturer to manufacture the goods, but before he starts the work, any one of the parties may cancel the contract after giving notice to the other.

But after the manufacturer has started the work, the contract cannot be cancelled unilaterally.

However, the party placing the order has the right to retract if the commodity does not conform to the specifications demanded.

Istisna as a Mode of Financing: can be used for providing the facility of financing in certain transactions, especially in the sector of house financing.

If the client has his own land and he seeks financing for the construction of a house, the financier may undertake to construct the house on that open land, on the basis of *Istisna*, and if the client has no land and he wants to purchase the land also, the financier may undertake to provide him a constructed house on the specified piece of land.

Since it is not necessary in *Istisna* that the price is paid in advance, nor is it necessary that it is paid at the time of the delivery, rather, it may be deferred to any time according to the agreement of the parties, therefore, the time of payment may be fixed in whatever manner they wish. The payment may also be in installments.

On the other hand, it is not necessary that the financier himself construct the house. He can enter into a parallel contract of *Istisna* with a third party, or may hire the services of a contractor (other than the client). In both cases, he can calculate his cost and fix the price of *Istisna* with his client in a manner that may give him a reasonable profit over his cost. The payment of installments by the client may start, in this case, right from the day when the contract of *Istisna* is signed by the parties, and may continue during the construction of the house and after it is handed over to the client. In order to secure the payments of installments, the bank, as a security, may keep the title deeds of the house or land, or any other property, until the client pays the last installment. The bank, in this case, will be responsible for the construction of the house in full conformity with the specifications detailed in the agreement. In case of discrepancy, the financier will undertake such alterations at his own cost as may be necessary for bringing it in harmony with the terms of the contract.

The instrument of *Istisna* may also be used for project

financing on similar lines. If a client wants to install machinery in his factory, and the machinery needs to be manufactured, the financier may undertake to prepare the machinery through the contract of *Istisna* according to the aforesaid procedure. The same principles will be fully applicable to the construction of a building for the industry.

Istisna contracts open wide fields of application for the Islamic banks to finance the public needs and the vital interests of the society to develop the Islamic economy. *Istisna* contracts are applied in high technology industries such as the aircraft industry, locomotive and ship building industries, in addition to the different types of machines produced in large factories or workshops. The *Istisna* contract is also applied in the construction industry for apartment buildings, hospitals, schools, and universities.

Difference between Istisna and Salam:[1](Usmani & Zubairi, 2002, pp. 131-132)

[1] Mufti Taqi Usmani ,Forward Sales and Manufacturing Contracts: Salam And Istisna. Available at: http://www.albalagh.net/Islamic_economics/salam_istisna.shtml

1. The subject of *Istisna* is always a thing that needs manufacturing, while *Salam* can be effected on anything, no matter whether it needs manufacturing or not.

2. It is necessary for *Salam* that the price is paid in advance, while it is not necessary in *Istisna.*

3. The contract of *Salam*, once effected, cannot be cancelled unilaterally, while the contract of *Istisna* can be cancelled before the manufacturer starts the work.

4. The time of delivery is an essential part of the sale in *Salam* while it is not necessary in *Istisna* that the time of the delivery be fixed.

5. The buyer may stipulate in the *Istisna* contract that the commodity shall be manufactured or produced by a specific manufacturer, or manufactured from specific materials. This is not permitted in the case of *Salam* sale.

Difference Between Istisna and Ijarah :[1](Usmani & Zubairi, 2002, pp. 132-133)

It should also be kept in mind that the manufacturer, in

---

[1] Mufti Taqi Usmani ,Forward Sales and Manufacturing Contracts: Salam And Istisna. Available at: http://www.albalagh.net/Islamic_economics/salam_istisna.shtml

Istisna, undertakes to make the required goods with his own material. Therefore, this transaction implies that the manufacturer shall obtain the material, if it is not already with him, and shall undertake the work required for making the ordered goods with it.

However, if the customer provides the material, and the manufacturer is required to use his labor and skill only, the transaction is not *Istisna*. In this case it will be a transaction of *Ijarah* whereby the services of a person are retained for a specified fee paid to him.

D. Islamic bonds (Sukuk) :

Muslim jurists subject the buying and selling of debt obligations to certain conditions in order to comply with the prohibition of *riba* (interest), *gharar* (uncertainty), and *maysir* (gambling). specify these conditions in detail. In summary, the debt must be a genuine one i.e., it must not be a subterfuge to borrow money such as an asset-linked buy-back arrangement. The debtor must acknowledge the trade and creditors must be known, accessible, and sound. Trading must be on a spot basis and not against debt. Importantly, the price cannot be other than the face value. In line with these principles, early doctrine on interest-free finance disallowed corporate or government bonds and the discounting of bills. Pressures for innovation have resulted in finding a way out of these limitations, admitting 'financial engineering'. In particular, leasing-based bonds (*sukuk al-ijara)* have been developed. Although other *sukuk* have been issued, eg *sukuk al-mudaraba, sukuk al-musharaka, sukuk al- murabaha,* the *ijara sukuk* remains the most popular.

Sukuk means participation certificate, and is commonly referred to as an 'Islamic bond'. Techniques similar to conventional structured finance securities are employed, with *sukuk* akin to pass-through certificates. A *sakk* simply represents a proportional or undivided ownership interest in an asset or pool of assets . Islamic bonds are more useful if they can be traded

on the secondary market to gain liquidity. As indicated above,certain requirements must be met with respect to the trading capacity of the bonds on the Islamic financial market. Specifically, they cannot represent a debt (in Islam, debt-selling is forbidden), as conventional bonds can. Instead they must constitute property of an approved asset. Such a bond is obtained through the securitization of the asset, the property of which is divided into equally valued units and incorporated in the *sukuk* certificates. The value of the *sukuk* thus remains connected to the value of the underlying asset. While they come in zero coupon and coupon versions, the productivity and return is linked to the profit of the underlying asset and not to an interest rate (although an interest rate such as LIBOR can be used as a 'benchmark').

Consider, for example, the case of the *sukuk al-ijara*. The originator holds assets (land, buildings, aircraft, ships, etc) that are to constitute the basis of the returns to the *sukuk* investor. These assets are sold by the originator to a special purpose vehicle (SPV) and then are leased back at a specified rental. The SPV securitizes the assets by issuing *sukuk* certificates that can be purchased by investors. Each *sukuk*In what ways does Islamic banking differ from conventional finance?

certificate represents a share in the ownership of the assets, entitling the investor to periodic distributions from the SPV funded by the originator's rental payments on the leased assets.

The returns can be either fixed rate or floating rate (often referenced to LIBOR as a 'benchmark') depending on the originator.

So far, AAOIFI (the Accounting and Auditing Organization for Islamic Financial Institutions) has issued Standards for fourteen types of *sukuk* .These can be broadly grouped into *sukuk* that bear predetermined returns and *sukuk* that allow for sharing of profit and, in some instances, loss. *Sukuk al-murabaha* and *sukuk al-murabaha* are examples of profit-and-loss-sharing *sukuk*. To date, most issued *sukuk* have borne predetermined returns, and the majority of such *sukuk* have been *sukuk al-ijara*, frequently at a predetermined rate of return.

In fact, the basic structure of a *sukuk* is very flexible and can be varied in a number of ways. The underlying assets that are pooled and securitized can be *ijara, murabaha, istisnaa* or *musharaka* receivables, or combinations of them, and the rates of return can be fixed, floating or zero coupon. Investment risks (credit risk, interest rate risk, foreign exchange risk, market price risk, liquidity risk) are much the same as those of conventional bonds, and depend on the way the securitization is structured, although one unique risk is that of *shari'a* compliance, a factor which also governs the tradeability of the *sukuk*.

Indeed, it is the potential for tradeability that primarily makes for the popularity of *sukuk al-ijara. Ijara*, though less commonly employed than *murabaha* as an asset in Islamic banks' balance sheets offers much greater flexibility for the Islamic bond market. Each security called *sukuk-al-ijara* represents a pro rata ownership of physical assets as against a pro rata share in financial claims or debt in the case of *sukuk-al-murabaha*. While debt can only be transferred at par, ownership in physical assets can always be transferred at a mutually negotiated price. Hence *sukuk-al-ijara* allow for creation of a secondary market since they represent a share in the ownership of a physical asset.

Total global sukuk issuance volume came in at USD119.7bln in 2013, 8.9% lower than 2012. The global primary sukuk market continues to be driven by robust infrastructure funding requirements,particularly in the GCC, the still accommodative monetary policy that makes sukuk an attractive asset class relative to conventional bonds, and strong demand for quality papers to meet regulatory requirements.(Rasameel Structured Finance, 2014)

Global outstanding sukuk reached USD269.4bln as at end-2013, increasing by 17.5% y-o-y (year-over-year return) from USD229.3bln as at end-2012. Only Kuwait and Pakistan saw y-o-y declines in secondary market size, while Turkey, Saudi Arabia and Indonesia were among the markets with the largest growth. The Malaysian secondary market, which accounts for 58.7% of the global industry, meanwhile witnessed modest growth of 10.0% in 2013 to reach USD158.3bln.(Rasameel Structured Finance, 2014)

Sourse:(Rasameel Structured Finance, 2014)

Global sukuk issuances continued to lean towards the short-term end in 2013, with the Fed taper being the major driver for this. Since May borrowing costs have risen, persuading issuers to shorten maturities for cheaper cost of funds. A prime example of this is the Indonesian sovereign US dollar sukuk issued in September 2013, with USD1.5bln raised at 6.125% over 5.5 years. This compares to the USD1bln raised in November 2012 at 3.3% over a 10-year maturity. Depending on interest rate movements moving forward, issuers, in particularly corporates, will need to evaluate the affordability of potential long and short-term issuances.(Rasameel Structured Finance, 2014)

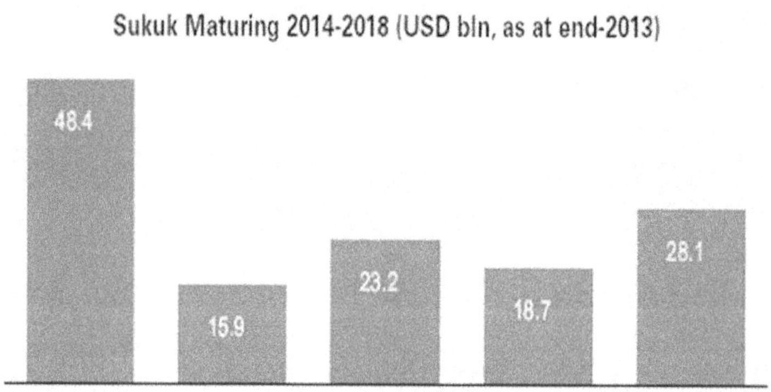

Finally, Islam has laid down a number of conditions to ensure that credit expands in step with the growth of the real rector. Some of these conditions are:

1. The asset which is being sold or leased must be real, and not imaginary or notional;

2. The seller must own and possess the goods being

sold or leased;

3. The transaction must be a genuine trade transaction with the full intention of giving and taking delivery; and

4. The debt cannot be sold and thus the risk of default associated with it must be borne by the lender himself.

The first condition will help eliminate most of the speculative and gambling transactions which involve notional goods and which constituted a major part of the derivatives transactions during the current crisis. The second condition will help ensure that the seller (or lessor) also shares a part of the risk to be able to get a share in the return. Once the seller (financier) acquires ownership and possession of the goods for sale or lease, he/she bears the risk. This condition will put a constraint on short sales, and thereby remove the possibility of a steep decline in asset prices during a downturn. The *Shari'ah* has, however, made an exception to this rule in the case of *salam* and *istisna* where the goods are not already available in the market and need to be produced or manufactured before delivery. This will help ensure that financing expands in step with the rise of the real economy and thereby help curb excessive credit expansion.

The third and the fourth conditions will not only help eliminate a great deal of speculative and derivatives transactions where there is no intention of giving or taking delivery, but also motivate the creditor to be more cautious in evaluating the credit risk. This will prevent an unnecessary explosion in the volume and value of transactions and also help keep the rise in debt to be in step with the rise of the real economy. It will also release a greater volume of financial resources for the real sector and, thereby, help expand employment and self-employment opportunities and the production of need-fulfilling goods and services.

The discipline that Islam wishes to introduce in the financial system may not materialize unless the governments reduce their borrowing from the central bank to a level that is in harmony with the goal of price and financial stability. Even borrowing from the private sector should be primarily for development that will increase its ability to repay. Borrowing for meeting current spending needs to be avoided except in extreme circumstances. This is because borrowing does not eliminate the ultimate need for sacrifice.

Without this consciousness about the ultimate need for sacrifice, the need for borrowing is most likely to become path dependent .A number of objections may be raised here against these conditions. One of these is that hedging is a genuine need of the economy and the restrictions specified above may stand against it. Genuine hedging or insurance which is undertaken by a person or firm to provide protection against losses actually incurred has been recognized by Muslim jurists. However, what is prohibited is 'hedging' that is not related to a real transaction and is rather of a speculative and gambling nature. A second objection may be that all these conditions will tend to shrink the size of the economy by reducing the number and volume of derivatives transactions. There is not doubt that the number of transactions will be reduced. However, it will be primarily those transactions which are of a speculative and gambling nature and are generally recognized to be zero-sum games. These have rarely contributed significantly to total real output. The compounded annual rate of growth of total outstanding derivatives between 2000 and 2007 was 29.9 percent per annum while that in total real world output was only 3.1 percent per annum. Hence a decline in speculative and gambling transactions is not likely to hurt the real economy significantly. While a restriction on such transactions will cut the commissions earned by speculators during an artificially generated boom, it will help them avert losses and bankruptcy that become unavoidable during the decline and lead to a financial crisis.

E. ISLAMIC BANKING

The emergence of Islamic banking in recent years is one of the most important trends in the economic sector, and with the estimated 1.6 billion Muslims worldwide, it's ripe for growth potential.

There has always been a demand among Muslims for financial products and services that conform to

Shari'ah(Islamic Law). The development of viable alternatives to conventional finance increasingly enables Muslims to participate in the financial world without violating their Islamic principles and without bearing the economic penalty that comes from non-participation, especially with the recent growth of oil prices.

Currently, the Islamic banking industry consists of several hundred billion dollars, and more than 300 financial institutions in and outside the Muslim world. There is $300 billion in assets managed according to Islamic principles, ranging from commercial to investment banks and investment funds, all providing Islamic products.[1]

Others estimate the industry to be even larger. Financial Services Authority, the financial services regulator in the United Kingdom, for example, recently suggested Islamic banking was as large as $500 billion. Standard & Poor's, a rating agency, estimates that the *sukuk* (deed) market has reached $70 billion, and will top the $160 billion mark by the end of the decade.(Al-Rifaee, 2008)

---

1 Sarah s. Al-Rifaee ,Islamic banking myths and facts.at:www.arabinsight.org

Islamic financial services are now evolving from a niche market to the mainstream.

In addition to the sheer number of Muslims worldwide, global financial institutions are taking a strong interest in Islamic products since the industry is in its nascent stage. Products have yet to be commoditized from competition, therefore allowing profit margins to remain high.

What is Islamic banking?

Islamic banking can be considered banking with a conscience. Islamic banks each have a Shari'ah board made up of Shari'ah scholars as well as financial experts who are responsible for determining what activities are and are not Shari'ah-compliant. Islamic banking is based on two main financial principles. Firstly, investment is to be made in the private sector through interest-free financing. Secondly, the development of financial instruments is to be done on the basis of profit and loss sharing as well as sharing risks.

Further, Islamic banking is built around Shari'ah, mainly

prohibiting the charging of interest. Because Islam considers interest an unjustified increase of capital, with no effort made to earn it, it is considered of false value, and therefore is prohibited. However, there are many arguments about the prohibition of interest in Islam. The first argument is that interest rates have no moral foundation. The second is that abstinence from consumption is not a justification of rewards.(Al-Rifaee, 2008)

Lastly, some argue that there are risks to justify the supplement of payment for capital lending if the loan is guaranteed.

In addition to the prohibition of interest payments, Islamic law treats money strictly as a medium of exchange. In other words, money, in itself, does not have any inherent value, and therefore it should not lead to the production of more money. In Islamic banking, the creditor/debtor relationship is defined differently than in the secular financial world. The creditor, or provider, of funds who becomes a partner in a project assumes the risk activity with the entrepreneur and shares profits as well as losses.

The creation of incremental wealth justifies the share of profit between the borrower and the lender of money, but does not guarantee a fixed return.

Some of the principle instruments involved in the aforementioned form of resource mobilization include the following:Trade financing and cost-plus mark-up on traded goods (*murabaha*).Profit-sharing (*mudarabah*) and equity participation (*musharaka*) in which cost-sharing among partners is also included.

Rental on purchased equipment (*ijara*).

In recent years, many new Islamic financial products have been developed and are increasingly used in financial market activities, including equity and bond (sukuk and certificate of investment) trading and investment, takaful and re-takaful, Islamic syndicated lending,and investment in Islamic collective investment schemes and other wealth and asset management products including Islamic trust services (waqf).(Saidi, 2008)

Islamic banking portfolio using secondary financing instruments, The following are the main differential points between conventional banking and Islamic banking.(AHMAD, 1998)

Sr. No.	CONVENTIONAL BANKING	ISLAMIC BANKING
1	Money is a commodity besides medium of exchange and store of value. Therefore, it can be sold at a price higher than its face value and it can also be rented out.	Money is not a commodity though it is used as a medium of exchange and store of value. Therefore, it cannot be sold at a price higher than its face value or rented out.
2	Time value is the basis for charging interest on capital.	Profit on trade of goods or charging on providing service is the basis for earning profit.
3	Interest is charged even in case the organization suffers losses by using bank's funds. Therefore, it is not based on profit and loss sharing.	Islamic bank operates on the basis of profit and loss sharing. In case, the businessman has suffered losses, the bank will share these losses based on the mode of finance used (Mudarabah, Musharakah).
4	While disbursing cash finance, running finance or working capital finance, no agreement for exchange of goods & services is made.	The execution of agreements for the exchange of goods & services is a must, while disbursing funds under Murabaha, Salam & Istisna contracts.
5	Conventional banks use money as a commodity which leads to inflation.	Islamic banking tends to create link with the real sectors of the economic system by using trade related activities. Since, the money is linked with the real assets therefore therefore it contributes directly in the economic development.

In particular, Islamic banks are already serving 38 million customers globally, two-thirds of who reside in seven countries, Malaysia, Saudi Arabia, UAE, Qatar, Bahrain, Indonesia, and Turkey. One-fifth of the banking system assets across these countries have now transitioned to Islamic. In Saudi Arabia, supply push has seen share of Islamic banking cross 50percent of system assets.The global market for Islamic financial services, as measured by Shari'ah compliant assets, is estimated by TheCityUK to have increased in 2013, to a record $1,688bn.(UK Islamic finance secretariat UKIFS, 2013)

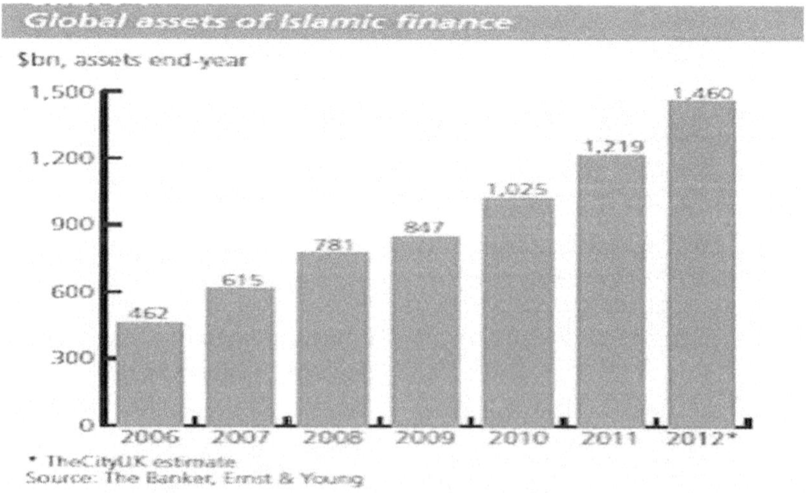

The industry is set to grow significantly in the years ahead. At the current rate of growth the market could top $2 trillion in assets by the end of 2014. The largest centres remain concentrated in Malaysia and the Middle East, including Iran, Saudi Arabia, UAE and Kuwait.

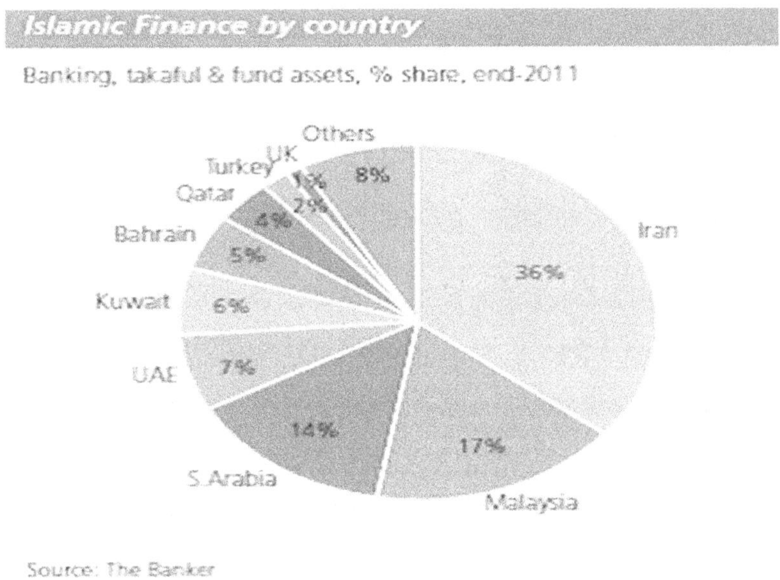

Islamic finance has shown resilience at a time when the global economy has slowed and conventional banking in Western countries has been under pressure. Global assets of Islamic finance have doubled since the start of the economic slowdown. Considerable potential exists for expansion of Islamic finance. The Muslim population numbering some 1.6 billion accounts for nearly a quarter of the global population, but Sharia compliant assets make up only around 1percent of the world's financial assets. Less than a fifth of Muslims worldwide currently use Islamic financial products. The extent of the industry's penetration varies substantially .There are over 700 institutions registered globally as sharia- compliant organisations in financial services. Of these, around 500 are full-fledged standalone institutions, and the remainder operate sharia-compliant products within a conventional institution or known as Islamic windows. Countries with most of the 430 firms reporting to The Banker's survey include Bahrain and Indonesia with 74 and 71 firms respectively. Malaysia, Iran, Kuwait and Saudi Arabia were in a group of countries with more than 50 firms.(UK Islamic finance secretariat UKIFS, 2013)

E. ISLAMIC CAPITAL MARKETS

Since 1990, the Islamic capital market has developed rapidly across the globe, from South- East Asia to the GCC region and to Europe,becoming a truly international market for fundraising activities. This strong growth has been driven by the increase in the earnings of oil exporting countries resulting from a rise in global oil prices. Participating institutions include multilateral organizations, such as the World Bank and the Islamic Development Bank (IDB), as well as both Islamic and conventional corporate entities. The Islamic capital market is an integral part of the Islamic financial system. It enables the efficient mobilization of resources and an optimal allocation thereof, thereby complementing the financial intermediary role of Islamic institutions in the investment process. Although this market functions similarly to the conventional capital market, any financial arrangement it facilitates has to be in line with the *Shari'ah* principles summarized earlier. At present, Islamic equity, Islamic bonds (*sukuk*),Islamic funds and Islamic real estate investment trusts (REITs) are offered as alternatives to conventional instruments.(Di Mauro et al., 2013)

III. Leading organizations of Islamic finance

In the beginning the industry focused all its attention on retail, which was followed by commercial banking activities. The next step, capital market activities, took a bit longer time to be developed, but it began to boom in a very short time and this boom attracted more and more actors into this business, especially western countries in the mid 1990s. As the Islamic finance industry attracted more and more countries and the public interest grew all over the world, central banks and regulatory authorities in these countries began to call for regulations and supervision of the Islamic finance industry. Another additional problem that followed the boom in IFIs was the difference in products available by these institutions. IFIs in the beginning of 1970s began increasingly to consult experts in Islamic law in order to be sure if their product were adherent to Shari'ah. However, there was need for a standard setting so the products at least could be of same content, if not the same name. All these problems led to the establishment of Shari'ah boards within the IFIs. But this was not enough because the inconsistencies in interpretations of different Shari'ah boards in IFIs led to the fact that some transactions were Shari'ah compliant in the rules of one board and not compliant with Shari'ah in the rules of other board. Therefore, international standard setting organs such as Accounting and Auditing Organization for Islamic Financial Institutions (AAOIFI), Islamic Financial Services Board (IFSB), Islamic International Rating Agency (IIRA), and International Islamic Financial Market (IIFM) were found to facilitate, by issuing international standards and guidelines, the homogeneous interpretation of Islamic jurisprudence and dealing with corporate governance issues. Recently the International Islamic Liquidity Management Corp (IILM) has been established to assist institutions offering Islamic financial services in addressing their liquidity management issues in an efficient and effective manner. These main bodies of Islamic finance are explained in detail in the following subchapters. (Faiz, 2011)

1. Shari'ah Boards

It should be stressed that Shari'ah board is not a standard setting body in itself, but assist other regulatory and standard setting organizations in establishing and maintaining a good governance practice among IFIs. Shari'ah board is a committee of Islamic scholars whose job is to verify if the new products presented by IFIs comply with Shari'ah. These scholars' functions are similar to members of boards in conventional corporations, i.e. they are not employed be IFIs but receive honoraria, and they have the right to be members of Shari'ah boards in different IFIs simultaneously. The latter is because there are few dozen countable Shari'ah scholars who are familiar with both Islamic law and modern financial needs in the world. Although the numbers of such scholars are growing, they still lag behind the growth of the industry need. The first ever Shari'ah board was established by

Egypt's Faisal Islamic Bank in 1976 and soon other IFIs followed this example. Today Shari'ah boards of IFIs are required by law in majority of Islamic countries, and even if it is not required by law, Shari'ah boards have become an important part of IFIs. However, lately Shari'ah boards have been criticized by many economists for being a part of corporate governance or agency theory problems in IFIs because of conflict of interests. To tackle these kinds of problems Malaysia as the first country in the world has regulated scholars to be member of the Shari'ah board of maximum three IFIs simultaneously. AAOIFI standards have defined Shari'ah boards' duty as directing, reviewing and supervising the activities of the IFIs in order to ensure that they are in compliance with Shari'ah principles. AAOIFI standards have also made it mandatory for all IFIs to elect their Shari'ah board members through the shareholders annual general meeting upon the recommendation of the board of directors, taking into consideration local legislation and regulations. Furthermore it states that these members should not be chosen among directors and majority shareholders of the

IFI. Maintaining and formalizing the internal regulatory role of Shari'ah boards is considered vital as these internal bodies are best placed to assist their individual organizations in achieving Shari'ah compliance, and thus play an important role in the overall regulatory environment. (Faiz, 2011)

2. AAOIFI

The Accounting and Auditing Organization for Islamic Financial Institutions (AAOIFI) is an Islamic international autonomous non-profit making corporate body that prepares accounting, auditing, governance, ethics and Shari'ah standards for Islamic financial institutions. It was established in accordance with the Agreement of Association which was signed by Islamic financial institutions on 26 February 1990 in Algiers. The AAOIFI has a two-tiered organizational structure in order to separate the standard-setting function from financing the organization, so that the standard setters are not subject to a conflict of interest. IFIs are not obliged to adapt AAOIFIs standards and guidelines. However, regulatory and supervisory authorities around the world are increasingly relying upon them and align their standards according to it. For example many Shari'ah boards consist of at least three scholars who have a comprehensive financial expertise and education in legal questions according to AAOIFI standards. The AAOIFI provides guidelines for IFIs when/if they face difficulties in interpretations, or understanding of issues related to new financial products. So far the AAOIFI has issued 25 standards in accounting, 5 in auditing, 7 in corporate governance and 2 codes of ethics. The AAOIFI is focusing on the auditing and accounting side, where processes and transactions need to be handled differently from conventional banking practice. (Faiz, 2011)

3. IFSB

To ensure the sound and stable development of the Islamic financial industry, it needs to be supported by a strong regulatory and supervisory framework. To fulfill this requirement, the Islamic Financial Services Board (IFSB) was established in 2002. The IFSB is an international body hosted by Malaysia. It has the important mandate of developing the prudential standards in accordance with the unique features of the Islamic financial institution. IFSB was established under the sponsorship of the International Monetary Fund, and in close cooperation with IMF and Basel Committee on Banking Supervision, has become one of the most influential international organizations that promote Islamic finance and its standards. IFSB tries to adapt the existing standards and guidelines of the mentioned organizations and adjusts them in accordance with the Shari'ah principles to IFIs. The IFSB's focus is very much on the standardization of procedures and the way Shari'ah rulings are interpreted across the industry. Since its establishment the IFSB has issued 17 standards, guiding principles and technical notes in the areas of risk management, corporate governance, transparency and market discipline, and etc. IFSB is closely cooperating with the Basel Committee on Banking Supervision, International Organization for Securities Commissions and the International Association of Insurance Supervisors.(Faiz, 2011)

4. IIRA

The Islamic International Rating Agency (IIRA) started operations in July 2005 to facilitate development of the regional and national financial markets by delineating relative investment or credit risk, providing an assessment of the risk profile of entities and instruments. This should be an integral part of the decision process employed by institutional investors. IIRA assists the Islamic financial services industry to gain recognition locally and internationally as strong and capable financial institutions, adhering to greater standards of disclosure and transparency. Its mission is to support the development of the regional capital market and to improve its functioning. IIRA has become an alternative to the international rating agencies and it aims to become a reference on which investors and financiers can rely to achieve "Quality" in terms of compliance with the related Shari'ah rules and principles for Islamic financial services. IIRA is a profit making body and it works like its conventional counterparts, charging a set fee per piece of work. (Faiz, 2011)

5. IIFM

International Islamic Financial Market (IIFM) is the global standardization body for the Islamic Capital & Money Market segment of the IFIs. Its primary focus lies in the standardization of Islamic financial products, documentation and related processes. The Agreement to establish the IIFM was signed in November 2001 by the Governors of the Central banks /Monetary Agencies Malaysia, Bahrain, Indonesia, Sudan, and the President of the Islamic Development Bank. It began its operation in 2002. Its main objectives are:

1. To spur the establishment and development of an international financial market based on Shari'ah rules and principles
2. Addressing the issue of liquidity management in IFIs
3. Developing an active secondary market, and
4. Creating the environment that will encourage both Islamic and non-Islamic financial institutions to actively participate in a

secondary market and the information of new traceable instructions.

IIFM will also act as the focal point for the harmonization of Shari'ah interpretations in the global financial market and enhance the cooperative framework among IFIs globally. In September 2006 the IIFM signed a Memorandum of Understanding with the International Swaps and Derivatives Association (ISDA), with an eye to developing a master agreement for documenting privately negotiated Shari'a-compliant derivatives transactions. In march 2010 the ISDA/IIFM Tahawwut master agreement was launched. It is a completely new framework document though the structure of the document is similar to the conventional ISDA Master Agreement. However, the key mechanisms and provisioning such as early termination events, closeout and netting are developed based on the Islamic Shari'ah principles.(Faiz, 2011)

6. IILM

I. The International Islamic Liquidity Management Corp (IILM) is a collaborative effort by 11 central banks or monetary agencies from countries such as

Malaysia, Indonesia, Iran, Luxembourg and the United Arab Emirates, as well as two multilateral organizations to assist institutions offering Islamic financial services in addressing their liquidity management. The IILM has been established to assist institutions offering Islamic financial services in addressing their liquidity management issues in an efficient and effective manner. This institution addresses one of the fundamental problems of Islamic financial institutions: the provision of adequate liquidity in times of stress. The IILM is expected to issue high quality, triple A-rated liquid, tradable and low risk Shari'ah-compliant financial instruments at both the national level and across borders, to enhance the soundness and stability of the Islamic financial markets. The instruments of the IILM will be utilized in liquidity management as eligible collateral for interbank transactions and central bank financing, or through trading of IILM instruments (either within the same country or cross border) in the secondary market. As the IILM is intended to facilitate cross-border liquidity management, its instruments shall be denominated in major reserve currencies such as the US dollar and the euro. This is to ensure access to a large pool of global investors and broaden the range of its holders, thereby enhancing the prospects for active secondary market. If the assets can be traded through the IILM, then much fewer of these assets will be held by the institutions.

IV. Islamic Finance in the United States

In the United States, there is growing interest for Islamic finance and business opportunities for lenders. Some have suggested Islamic finance may be an attractive option for investors as conventional finance faces challenges from the U.S. subprime lending crisis and recession concerns. In the United States, *shariah*-compliant finance largely exists in personal home mortgages. Since its establishment in 2002, Guidance Residential , an Islamic home finance company,has provided over $1.5 billion in *shariah*-compliant home financing in the United States. Other financial intermediaries that provide Islamic-based home mortgages include University Islamic Financial, Devon Bank, and American Finance House Lariba. HSBC is the only large commercial bank that offers U.S. Islamic finance, and is focused on New York.. The Federal National Mortgage Association (Fannie Mae) and the Federal Home Mortgage Corporation (Freddie Mac) purchase *shariah*-compliant mortgage contracts from financial intermediaries, allowing providers to originate further mortgages. In 2007, Freddie Mac reportedly purchased more than $250 million in Islamic home loans, a small but notable fraction of the enterprise's $1.77 trillion in business activities. The Federal National Mortgage Association (Fannie Mae) and the Federal Home Mortgage Corporation (Freddie Mac) purchase *shariah*-compliant mortgage contracts from financial intermediaries, allowing providers to originate further mortgages. In 2007, Freddie Mac reportedly purchased more than $250 million in Islamic home loans, a small but notable fraction of the enterprise's $1.77 trillion in business activities.(Ilias, 2010)

Other forms of *shariah*-compliant services are offered in the United States as well. For instance,Devon Bank and Zayan Finance offer SCF for commercial real estate. *Shariah*-compliant mutual funds are offered by intermediaries such as the Amana Mutual Funds Trust, Azzad Funds, and the Dow Jones Islamic Fund. International financial intermediaries also provide SCF in the United States. Muslim investors from the countries of the Gulf Cooperation Council (GCC) have sought to diversify their financial portfolios geographically and to invest their wealth in U.S. assets. For instance, the Bahrain-based Arcapita Bank has structured *shariah*-compliant transactions in private equity and real estate in the United States. U.S.-based companies also have taken advantage of alternative funding sources through Islamic financing abroad. For example, in November 2009, General Electric became the first major U.S.company to sell an Islamic bond. It sold a five-year, $500 million Islamic bond in order to attract international investors who want to invest according to Islamic principles.(Ilias, 2010)

U.S. Policy Interests in Islamic Finance : (Ilias, 2010; Zyp, 2009)

As Islamic finance activities grow in the United States, critics raise concerns about the related capital adequacy and system risks. Proponents of Islamic finance assert that the ban on risk-taking mitigates many concerns. Some also view the integration of ethics and values into finance as a positive development, especially in light of recent U.S. business corruption scandals. Many investors reportedly consider *shariah*-compliant finance to be more resilient to global economic and financial crises than conventional finance. However, others point out that Islamic financial markets are still tied to the world economy and are not completely sheltered from the ups and downs of international markets. The growth of Islamic finance in the United States may have implications for congressional oversight. Congress may be interested in evaluating the relationship between the current U.S.banking legal and regulatory framework and Islamic finance. Current U.S.

laws and regulation may be broad enough to accommodate some aspects of Islamic finance. Others aspects of Islamic finance may pose some unique challenges to U.S. laws and regulations, such as applying rules created for conventional, interest-based products to Islamic products. There is debate about whether or not, or the extent to which, regulators should apply rules on conventional products to Islamic product counterparts.

Some U.S. financial institutions express concerns about the possible ties of some Islamic institutions to terrorist finance networks. According to this viewpoint, there is the possibility that Islamic banking transactions may channel funds to terrorists or enable terrorists to access funds. Others assert that the risks of Islamic finance are not significantly greater or different than those from conventional finance and that the majority of recent terrorist financing cases related to SCF have been thrown out of court. In congressional testimony, one observer stated "there is no reason—in theory—to suspect that Islamic finance would be particularly immune or particularly vulnerable to abuse by money launderers or terrorist financiers". Some proponents also assert that security-related concerns about Islamic finance stem from a lack of understanding of SCF or from stereotyping. There may be a "conflation" of Islamic finance

with *hawala*, an informal trust-based money transfer system prominent in the Middle East and many Muslim countries. *Hawala* transactions are based on an honor system, with no promissory instruments exchanged between the parties and no records of the transactions. Some analysts consider the *hawala* system particularly susceptible to terrorist financing.

V. Steps Forward-- Some Recommendations

Islamic financial markets are operating far below their potential because Islamic banking by itself cannot take root in the absence of the other necessary components of an Islamic financial system. A number of limitations will have to be addressed before any long-term strategy can be formulated: (Iqbal, 1997, 2007)

• A uniform regulatory and legal framework supportive of an Islamic financial system has not yet been developed. Existing banking regulations in Islamic countries are based on the Western banking model. Similarly, Islamic financial institutions face difficulties operating in non- Islamic countries owing to the absence of a regulatory body that operates in accordance with Islamic principles. The development of a regulatory and supervisory framework that would address the issues specific to Islamic institutions would further enhance the integration of Islamic markets and international financial markets.

• There is no single, sizable, and organized financial center that can claim to be functioning in accordance with Islamic principles. Although stock markets in emerging Islamic countries such as Egypt, Jordan, and Pakistan are active, they are not fully compatible with Islamic principles. The stock markets in Iran and Sudan may come closest to operating in compliance with Islamic principles. Moreover, the secondary market for Islamic products is extremely shallow and illiquid, and money markets are almost nonexistent, since viable instruments are not currently available. The development of an interbank market is another challenge.

• The pace of innovation is slow. For years, the market has offered the same traditional instruments geared toward shortand medium-term maturities, but it has not yet come up with the necessary instruments to handle maturities at the extremes. There is a need for risk-management tools to equip clients with instruments to hedge against the high volatility in currency and commodities markets. In addition, the market lacks the necessary instruments to provide viable alternatives for public debt financing.

• An Islamic financial system needs sound accounting procedures and standards. Western accounting procedures are not adequate because of the different nature and treatment of financial instruments. Well-defined procedures and standards are crucial for information disclosure, building investors' confidence, and monitoring and surveillance. Proper standards will also help the integration of Islamic financial markets with international markets. Islamic institutions have a shortage of trained personnel who can analyze and manage portfolios, and develop innovative products according to Islamic financial principles. Only a limited number of Islamic institutions can afford to train their staffs and deploy resources in product development.

• There is lack of uniformity in the religious principles applied in Islamic countries. In the absence of a universally accepted central religious authority, Islamic banks have formed their own religious boards for guidance. Islamic banks have to consult their respective religious boards, or *Shari'ah* advisors, to seek approval for each new instrument. Differences in interpretation of Islamic principles by different schools of thought may mean that identical financial instruments are rejected by one board but accepted by another. Thus, the same instrument may not be acceptable in all countries. This problem can be addressed by forming a uniform council representing different schools of thought to define cohesive rules and to expedite the process of introducing new products.

Improvement can be made in several areas to promote and enhance the providing Islamic financial services. However, certain areas deserve immediate attention.

A. Financial Engineering:

Financial engineering and financial innovations are driving the global financial system toward greater economic efficiency by expanding the opportunities for sharing risk, lowering transaction costs, and reducing asymmetric information and agency costs. Financial engineering involves the design, development, and implementation of innovative financial instruments and processes as well as the formulation of creative solutions. Financial engineering may lead to a new consumer-type financial instrument, or a new security, or a new process or creative solution to corporate finance problems, such as the need to lower funding costs, manage risk better, or increase the return on investments.

For Islamic financial institutions, a financial engineering challenge is to introduce new Shari'ah-compatible products that enhance liquidity, risk management, and portfolio diversification. Generally, attempts to apply financial engineering techniques to Islamic banking will require committing a great deal of resources to understanding the risk-return characteristics of each building block of the system and offering new products with different risk-return profiles that meet the demand of investors, financial intermediaries, and entrepreneurs for liquidity and safety. Securitization is a prime candidate for financial engineering. New financial innovations are also needed to satisfy the demand for instruments at both ends of the maturity structure: extremely short-term deposits and long-term investments. Money markets that are Shari'ah compatible do not exist at present, and there is no equivalent of an Islamic interbank market where banks could place, say, overnight funds or could borrow to satisfy a need for temporary liquidity. Although securitization of a pool of lease portfolios could help to develop the interbank market, the volume of transactions offered by securitization may not be sufficient to meet the demand.

Islamic financial institutions are, in general, of small size and cannot afford to invest substantial funds in research and development. They are unable to reap the benefits of economies Informal discussions with practitioners revealed that religious boards sometimes are extremely rigid on minor technical matters and make the process of introducing a new product difficult and lengthy, resulting in missed business opportunities. The importance of financial engineering, Islamic financial institutions should seriously consider making joint efforts to develop the basic infrastructure for introducing new products. Conducting basic research and development collectively may save some of the costs required to build this infrastructure individually. A good example of such collective effort would be to sponsor research in the development of analytical models, computer systems, and tools to analyze the risk and return on different instruments. Financial engineering is an area where Islamic financial institutions could benefit from more experienced Western institutions, which are more sophisticated in engineering and marketing the right product to the right client. Conventional investment banks, which have invested heavily in the infrastructure for developing new products, can work for or with Islamic financial institutions to develop Shari'ah-compliant products. (Chapra, 2007; Iqbal, 2007)

B. Risk Management and Diversification:

Due to limited resources, Islamic banks are often unable to afford high-cost management information systems or the technology to assess and monitor risk in a timely fashion. With weak management and lack of proper risk-monitoring systems, the risk exposure of Islamic banks is high.

Providing a more diverse mix of financial services or spreading risks over a larger geographic area imply at least the potential for improved diversification, so the same protection against financial distress can be attained with fewer resources. For Islamic financial institutions, geographic expansion of the depositor base could achieve diversification on the liabilities side. Diversification on the assets side could reduce the variance of the returns that accrue to claimholders of the financial intermediary. Also, geographic and sectoral diversification on the assets side could break up the financial institutions' concentration in a region or a sector and thus reduce its exposure by creating less perfectly correlated risks. Geographic spread of products can further help the financial intermediary to improve its credit risk by selecting borrowers with the best credit and avoiding those with the weakest. With diversification, Islamic banks would be able to extend the maturity frontier.

Islamic financial intermediaries need to adopt appropriate risk management not only for their own portfolio but also for that of their clients. Diversification and risk management are closely associated with the degree of market incompleteness. In highly incomplete markets, financial intermediaries are in a better position to provide diversification and risk management for the client because the responsibility for risk diversification shifts from the investors to the financial intermediary, which is considered to be better at providing intertemporal risk management. Islamic financial institutions need to take immediate steps to devise an infrastructure for implementing proper measures, controls, and management of risk and to create innovative instruments to share, transfer, and mitigate financial risk so that entrepreneurs can concentrate on what they do best: managing exposure to business risk in which they have a comparative advantage.

Finally, Islamic financial institutions need to realize the importance not only of financial risk and its management but also of operational risk, which is risk due to the failure of controls and processes. Currently, there is a serious lack of a risk culture and of enterprise-level sponsorship of active risk management. (Chapra, 2007; Iqbal, 2007)

C. Non-Bank Financial Services:

For further growth, the role of intermediation should be extended beyond its traditional setup. In particular, there is a need to broaden the scope and range of financial services offered, similar to the concept of a "financial products supermarket." Such a supermarket would act like an "all-in-bank" covering all sorts of financial services. In this role, the Islamic bank would serve as a one-stop shop catering to different types of customers, ranging from private individuals, institutions, high-net-worth individuals, and corporations and offering products that serve their investment, borrowing, risk management, and wealth management needs. For example, such an institution would serve retail customers, manage investment portfolios, and provide various services for corporate customers. At the same time, like a broker, the financial products supermarket would be a retail firm that manages assets and offers payment and settlement services. Most Islamic banks are not adequately equipped to provide typical investment banking services, such as underwriting, guarantees, market research, and fee-based advisory services. The refinement and development of fee-based services would enhance the functionality of Islamic financial services. Fee-based contracts like *joalah*, *wakalah*, and *kifalah* require further development if they are to be recognized and operationalized to exploit the full capabilities of Islamic banks.(Chapra, 2007; Iqbal, 2007)

D. Development of Capital Markets:

Responding to the current wave of oil revenues and growing demand for Shari'ah-compliant products, Islamic capital markets are expanding at a quickening pace, and stakeholders are starting to realize their potential. Development of institutional infrastructure, such as accounting standards and regulatory bodies, is a step in the right direction. However, the market needs host governments to undertake strong leadership and constructive policy actions.

Well-developed Islamic capital markets will not only benefit borrowers and institutional investors, they also can enhance the stability of Islamic banks, providing them with improved portfolio, liquidity, and risk management tools. Ultimately, these developments will help to integrate Islamic financial markets, as well as the institutions that form them, into the broader conventional international financial system.

On the supply side, the volume of Islamic investments, with a preference for Shari'ah-compliant instruments, has grown to form a critical mass that can support a well-functioning and efficient capital market. It is evolving into a truly international market. Not only highly rated borrowers, such as the multilateral development banks (for example, the World Bank), but also developing-country borrowers with lower credit ratings, such as Pakistan, have successfully raised a considerable volume of funds in this market.

These institutions include the IFSB, AAOIFI, Liquidity Management Center, International Islamic Financial Markets, and International Islamic Rating Agency. On the demand side, countries in the developing world, especially the middle-income countries, will require a significant volume of investments in infrastructure over the next decade. For Indonesia alone, additional infrastructure investments of $5 billion (2 percent of GDP) are required annually, to reach a 6 percent medium-term growth target . Because the domestic capital markets of these borrowers are often too shallow to satisfy their large investment needs, they will have to access external sources of financing.

Furthermore, Muslim stakeholders in middle-income countries are increasingly expressing their preference for Shari'ah-compliant financing. In turn, financial intermediaries, including private sector commercial and investment banks, as well as development finance institutions, will have to start paying more attention to the "non-financial" needs of their clients.

For the multilateral development banks, the development of Islamic capital markets is a highly relevant topic. First, multilateral development banks are deeply involved in infrastructure finance and are naturally interested in the Islamic capital market as a new and alternative source of financing. Second, by channeling the funds available in Islamic financial markets, which are mostly based in the countries with high savings such as the Gulf Cooperation

Council countries and Malaysia, to finance investments in developing countries, multilateral development banks can create a new model for international cooperation while responding to the stakeholders' voices on both sides. Third, multilateral development banks can promote financial stability by encouraging the development of Islamic capital markets and providing the momentum to integrate the Islamic financial markets into the international financial system.

In the near future, structures such as *ijarah* (a lease) and *murabahah* (a cost-plus sales contract used to purchase commodities) that provide investors with a predetermined return as well as full recourse to the obligor probably will have more market potential than other structures. This will be driven primarily by investor preferences, but a large proportion of potential borrowers will prefer to lock in their borrowing costs rather than engage in pure profit-sharing schemes. While the future appears promising, certain obstacles lie ahead, and market participants and regulators need to take concrete steps to support market takeoff. First and most important, market development requires strong sponsorship and leadership on the part of the host-country government, especially regarding legal and regulatory issues. For example, for an *ijarah* transaction, the owner of operating assets enters into a leasing transaction. While the owner of operating assets is often the government itself or related public sector bodies, the relevant laws and regulations in the host country may not allow these bodies to pledge or lease assets needed to structure an *ijarah* transaction. This is a fundamental point; the host country's policy actions are a key prerequisite for further market development.

In addition, borrowers, investors, and intermediaries need to nurture the market patiently. Islamic transactions are often less cost-efficient than conventional bond issues. Each new issue incurs higher legal and documentary expenses as well as distribution costs because it involves examining structural robustness in addition to evaluating the credit quality of the obligor. Since the terms available in Islamic capital markets are derived mostly from pricing levels in the more liquid conventional bond markets, there is no inherent cost advantage for borrowers tapping

Islamic markets. Borrowers, therefore, need to formulate a comprehensive, long-term, and strategic view on how to reduce the overall cost of tapping Islamic markets, rather than focus on a single transaction. Investors can support market development by expressing their preference for *Shari'ah*-compliant instruments, namely, in their bid prices. Intermediaries can lead the process, perhaps through further standardization of transaction schemes and instruments.(Chapra, 2007; Iqbal, 2007)

E. Corporate social responsibility in Islam

Corporate Social Responsibility (CSR) is a concept that has attracted worldwide attention and acquired a new resonance in the global economy. Heightened interest in CSR in recent years has stemmed from the advent of globalization and international trade ،which have reflected in increased business complexity and new demands for enhanced transparency and corporate citizenship. Moreover, while governments have traditionally assumed sole responsibility for the improvement of the living conditions of the population, society's needs have exceeded the capabilities of governments to fulfill them. In this context, the spotlight is increasingly turning to focus on the role of business in society and progressive companies are seeking to differentiate themselves through engagement in CSR.(Jamali & Mirshak, 2007)

Corporate Social Responsibility CSR is an idea that has been constantly evolving as business firms are continually more aware of the community around them. CSR encompasses a business firm's obligation to society beyond simply maximizing its profits . CSR was not taken seriously and sometimes mocked by business firms before the late 1970s.The change in approach toward CSR can be partially attributed to the enactment of new legislation that created many of the regulatory government agencies during this time period. The new legislation provided business firms with an added incentive to earmark appropriate amounts of fiscal resources to CSR, rather than face harsh government regulation. The attitude toward CSR changed drastically by the late 1990s, as CSR was now a mainstream idea being promoted by different facets of society, ranging from corporations to governments.(Brown, 2013)

Corporate social responsibility (CSR) has grown enormously in the last thirty years and most business organizations feel to give in charity. The business organizations involving charitable giving and reflecting the highly competitive environment of the 1990s has been termed "strategic charity". It involves corporate giving which serves dual purposes: contributing funds to charitable causes while simultaneously benefiting the firm's financial bottom line and enhancing business political legitimacy. "Strategic charity" has become an accepted practice that allows a corporation to satisfy altruistic impulses to contribute in charitable causes while serving the bottom line. In this way the corporate community investment has emerged through the objectives of CSR programmes and business organizations some times take care of neighbor through its philanthropic responsibility programmes. Pure charity is concerned with assistance to education, arts and culture, health and social services, civic and community projects. While "strategic charity" combines pure philanthropy and business sponsorship with giving programmes that are directly or indirectly linked to business objectives. One of the characteristics of the "strategic charity" is a joint sponsorship of one or more corporations' programmes to implement through purposefully created charity foundations in order to optimize the charity value.(Hassan & Latiff, 2009)

Over the past 50 years, business ethicists and management theorists have devoted much effort to thinking through the business-society relationship . These ethicists developed models that could be modified or compromised to suit evolving social interests. In general there are six major ethical models that now dominate ethical thinking leading to the concept of corporate social responsibility. These can be summarized as following: (Mohammed, 2007)

1. **Relativism** – Ethical decisions are made on the basis of self-interest and needs, excluding any interaction with or input from the outside.

2. **Utilitarianism** – Ethical decisions are made on the basis of calculating costs and benefits. Utilitarianism is generally considered outcome oriented. Whatever is good for majority is considered ethical.

3. **Universalism** – Ethical decisions stress on the intention of the decision or action (duty). Everyone under similar circumstances should reach similar decisions.

4. **Rights** – Ethical decisions stress a single value - liberty, and are based on individual rights (individual entitlement) ensuring freedom of choice.

5. **Distributive Justice** – Ethical decisions revolve around a single value – justice. To be considered ethical, decisions and actions should ensure an equitable distribution of wealth and benefits (fairness and equality).

6. **Eternal Law** – Ethical decisions are made on the basis of eternal law, which is revealed in scripture.

These ethical models provide a background to the concept of corporate social responsibility. There have been efforts to conceptualize ethical behavior in terms of business practices of corporations in society. Much of this work has specifically focused on theorizing what responsibility corporations have to society and what the consequences of related actions or inactions are.

CSR literature identifies several driving forces behind the growing trend towards CSR initiatives: (Wajdi Dusuki, 2008)

1. There is growing market pressure, wherein customers, employees, or capital markets exert some form of preference, pressure or signal. Social and ethical issue shave received increasing public attention and affected market performance, in addition to the traditional price and brand preferences. The growth of the ethical investment industry is another indicator of how much emphasis

people are now apparently placing on the social and ethical behavior of companies.

2. There has been an increasing regulatory pressure ranging from reporting requirements to government regulations that introduce compulsory business standards by which companies of all sizes have to abide.

3. Increased power of communications (e.g. internet, electronic media, and others) have driven consumers and pressure groups like social activists, non-governmental organizations (NGOs) and trade unions to scrutinize the activities of companies more effectively and develop strategies that may influence companies to act in a socially responsible way.

4. There is a competitive advantage that companies believe they can reap by being socially responsible. They foresee that by communicating effectively about their social, environmental and economic contributions, they can strengthen their brand,

enhance their corporate reputation with customers and suppliers, and attract and retain a committed and skilled workforce. Indeed, extant literature asserts that, the commitment to CSR will in turn lead to better performance in terms of profitability, competitiveness and risk management.

The influence of Islam on business practices are well documented in the Holy Qur"an and Sunah , which are the main sources of business ethics in Islam. Islamic business values such as justice, socio-economic measure, human well-being, honesty etc are considered as the core of CSR in Islam. Islamic financial Institutions (IFIs) are considered as having an ethical identity and they have different social and economic objectives since the foundation of their business is based on religion .(Ali Aribi & Gopinath Arun, 2012; Haniffa & Hudaib, 2007; Maali, Casson, & Napier, 2006)

The general objective of IFIs is to contribute to the development of the economy within the boundary of

Islam. Within the range of Shari'a (Islamic law), IFIs are expected to be guided by an Islamic economic worldview, which is based on the principle of social justice and the well-being of society.(Wajdi Dusuki, 2008)

Islamic Financial Institution (IFI) are like any other conventional financial institution, which acts as an intermediary between providers of funds and fund users, the only difference being that the transactions and contracts of an IFI must comply with Islamic law.

Growing awareness of and demand for investing in accordance with Islamic ethical principles on a global scale have been catalyst towards making the Islamic banking and financial system as a flourishing industry. This is also a reflection of increasing wealth and capacity of investors, both Muslim and non-Muslim, to seek and invest in new investment products that serves their needs. The Islamic financial institutions (IFIs) earn profits as the other business firms earn profits. Many people say that IFIs should have involved "strategic charity" activities. Business of IFIs including Islamic banks is based on Shari'ah principles which need the IFIs to operate with the commitment of social responsibility.(Hassan & Latiff, 2009)

In the context of IFIs, the Association of Accounting and Auditing Organization for Islamic Financial Institutions (AAOIFI) has issued specific standards on CSR known as Governance Standards No. 7: Corporate Social Responsibility, Conduct and Disclosure for IFIs. According to the (AAOIFI), Corporate Social Responsibility (CSR) for IFIs refers to all activities carried out by an IFI[1] to fulfill its religious, economic, legal, ethical and discretionary responsibilities as financial intermediaries for individuals and institutions. Religious responsibility refers to the overarching obligation of IFIs to obey the laws of Islam in all its dealings and operations. Economic responsibility refers to the obligation for Islamic banks to be financially viable, profitable and efficient. Legal

[1] The IFIs referred to any institution that plays the role of a financial intermediary that strictly abides by the provisions of the Shari'a. These include, but are not limited to Islamic banks and Islamic Insurance companies.

responsibility refers to the obligation of IFIs to respect and obey the laws and regulations of the country of operation. Ethical responsibility refers to the obligation of IFIs to respect the mass of societal, religious and customary norms which are not codified in law. Discretionary responsibility refers to the expectation from stakeholders that IFIs will perform a social role in implementing Islamic ideals over and above the religious, economic, legal and ethical responsibilities.(AAOIFI, n.d.)

Indeed, the founding fathers of modern day Islamic finance have concurred to the view that IFIs do have a heightened sense of social responsibility, as do any other 'Islamic' institution. However, this does not entail IFIs to become uncompetitive and unprofitable charitable organizations used to only further social development objectives. This entails a change in the mindset of Islamic bankers to incorporate social development objectives into their portfolio of investments profitably. As more investment account holders, shareholders and general stakeholders understand fully the objectives that underlie the Islamic economic system, there shall be more demand to know to what extent their local IFI fulfils those social objectives. Therefore, the IFI that extensively involves itself in CSR and demonstrates by disclosure that it is extensively involved in CSR will more easily earn the legitimacy of certain stakeholders (particularly those interested in the IFIs CSR activities), and ultimately earn their loyalty. This represents in itself a value proposition for IFIs who seek to retain clients on the basis of non-price competition. However, this is not to say that IFIs should implement corporate social responsibility because of its long term economic benefits. While viable economic institutions have to be driven by profit incentives, in the case of IFIs, it is not their only priority and certainly not the only reason for them to implement corporate social responsibility. Indeed, any notion that IFIs or any other institution that claims to be Islamic, for that matter, should be socially responsible must derive its justification from Islamic law and principles, as contained within the Qur'an and the *Sunnah* of the Prophet of Islam, Muhammad (P.B.U.H). Without this ultimate source of legitimacy, there is no reason for any action.(Farook 2007)

ICSR derives itself from core principles in the holy Qur'an. The three major foundational principles for ICSR are the vicegerency of mankind on earth, divine accountability and the duty on mankind to enjoin good and forbid evil.(Farook 2007)

According to

F. ***Vicegerency***

The principle of vicegerency denotes that mankind is the representative of Allah on earth and as such Allah has entrusted mankind with stewardship of Allah's possession.

G. ***Divine Accountability***

The principle of divine accountability flows from the vicegerency principle and denotes that individuals will be accountable to Allah for all of their actions on the Day of Judgment. This principle is expounded in several verses of the holy Qur'an. This divine accountability is the basis for all actions of a Muslim, and in turn the representative organizations of Muslims.

H. *Enjoining Good and Forbidding Evil*

The principle of enjoining good and forbidding evil encapsulates the responsibilities that Allah places on Muslims as trustees and vicegerents.

This responsibility is overwhelming and encompasses all aspects of a Muslim's life. It comprises a prescription towards positive (permissible and recommended) actions and a prescription against negative (impermissible and not recommended) actions. IFIs have generally ensured their operational status by avoiding negative actions. However, their approach to positive actions has been varied due to a lack of standards in the area.

The combination of these principles denotes a divine accountability for each Muslim to enjoin good and justice and forbid evil and injustice. These core principles therefore constitute the basis of individual social responsibility.

Milton Friedman is one of the architects of the movement against social responsibility, writing what is considered by many the seminal piece of work disparaging CSR and the businesses who promoting their CSR credentials.(Milton Friedman, 1962, 1982; Milton Friedman, September 13, 1970)

Friedman's objection to CSR was two-fold.(Moon, 2011) First, he argued that managers were accountable to the owners of the business and that,unless they otherwise signalled, the assumption should be that the owners wanted the

profits of the company to be maximised. The corollary is that for Friedman CSR is a net expenditure with no positive benefits for the company. Somewhat curiously, he added that it was possible for companies to make community investments but if these had some company advantages (e.g. workforce loyalty, productivity), they should not be considered as CSR. The conclusion here is that Friedman did not regard social and private Interests as potentially in conformance - rather they are dichotomous. This will betaken up later in the paper underthe heading, the 'socialisation of markets'.

Secondly, Friedman argued that CSR encroached on the proper terrain of (democratic) government and that managers are neither trained in addressing public policy questions and thus lack appropriate expertise, nor are they accountable for public policy issues. In both cases the contrast is made with legislators and public servants, both of whom he sees as having expertise and being properly accountable. In short, Friedman (1970) offers

another dichotomy, in this case between the work of government and the business of business.

F. Corporate governance in Islamic Finance

Corporate governance aims at providing institutions with a body of rules and principles, with a view to ensuring that

good practices guide overall management of an institution. It has now come to mean the whole process of managing a company and the incentive structure to address principal-agent issues and ensure that executive management serves the long-term best interests of the shareholders and sustainable
value of the company in conformity with the laws and ethics of the country. All of the complex factors that are involved in balancing the power between the chief executive officer (CEO), the board, and the shareholders are now considered to be a part of the corporate
governance framework, including auditing, balance sheet and off-balance disclosure, and transparency.(Saidi, 2008)
If Islamic financial institutions are to be credible to their clients, they need to have a formalised system to ensure that all their activities are Shari'ah compliant. Exactly what constitutes an effective Shari'ah governance system is a matter of debate, however, and it is apparent from examining the experiences of different countries and institutions that a variety of systems are in place. This pluralistic approach has advantages, as the legal

environments in which Islamic financial institutions operate differ, not only in terms of the status of Shari'ah, but also depending on whether the countries use common or civil law. Furthermore, client expectations of what constitutes acceptable and effective Shari'ah governance differ, and, as will be evident from this study, most systems currently employed are market rather than state driven. Indeed, in the realm of Islamic finance, Shari'ah governance has largely been privatised rather than nationalised.The credibility of financial institutions with their clients has been highlighted by the financial crisis of 2008, when some conventional financial institutions faced a run on deposits. Many conventional financial institutions found that they had lost the confidence of other banks and, hence, they could no longer rely on the inter-bank market for funding. Merely having a Shari'ah Board does not, of course, provide immunity to liquidity crises or overcome the difficulties associated with the credit crunch, but it was noticeable that in many jurisdictions Islamic banks fared better than their conventional counterparts. (Wilson, 2009) This was because of two factors that were positively linked to Shari'ah governance. Firstly, Islamic banks have to rely on depositors rather than inter-bank borrowing for their funding, which immunized them from the credit crunch. However, their ability to continue to harness these funds depends on the depositor's perceptions of the integrity of the Shari'ah governance system. Secondly, Islamic banks could not hold assets that would ultimately prove toxic–for instance, credit derivative swaps or collateralised debt obligations–as such assets are not Shari'ah compliant, and their acquisition would not have been approved by any Shari'ah Board.

In other words, although the management of credit, liquidity, operational and other risks is the responsibility of the Board of Directors of an Islamic bank and not the Shari'ah Board, good Shari'ah governance prevents financial institutions from damaging themselves. In essence, this financial crisis, like others before it, was caused by human greed and uncontrolled excesses. Such behavior has no place in Islamic finance, and it is effective Shari'ah governance that promotes moderation and justice in financial transactions.

The agency problem arises because of the relationship between the owners and the management. The scandal in corporate governance made the scholars defining corporate governance based on the problem solving perspective or corporate affairs perspective. In addition, most definition states that internal governance mechanism involves board of directors and ownership structure while external involves to take over market and legal system.

The governments of the 30 OECD countries have approved a revised version of the OECD's Principles of Corporate Governance adding new recommendations for good practice in corporate behaviour with a view to rebuilding and maintaining public trust in companies and stock markets.

The revised Principles respond to a number of issues that have undermined the confidence of investors in company management in recent years. They call on governments to ensure genuinely effective regulatory frameworks and on companies themselves to be truly accountable. They advocate an increased awareness among institutional investors and an effective role for shareholders in executive compensation. They also urge strengthened transparency and disclosure to counter conflicts of interest.

Corporate governance aims at providing institutions with a body of rules and principles, with a view to ensuring that good practices guide overall management of an institution. It has now come to mean the whole process of managing a company and the incentive structure to address principal-agent issues and ensure that executive management serves the long-term best interests of the shareholders and sustainable value of the company in conformity with the laws and ethics of the country. All of the complex factors that are involved in balancing the power between the Chief Executive Officer (CEO), the board, and the shareholders are now considered to be a part of the corporate governance framework, including auditing, balance sheet and off-balance disclosure, and transparency.

Hence, corporate governance refers to the method by which a corporation is directed, administered and controlled. It includes the laws and customs affecting that direction, as well as the goals for which it is governed. Corporate governance mechanisms, incentives and controls are designed to reduce the inefficiencies that arise from moral hazard and adverse selection. Corporate governance is also viewed as a process of monitoring performance by applying appropriate counter- measures and dealing with transparency, integrity and accountability. It organizes the way corporations are accountable to shareholders and the public, and also the monitoring of the executive management of organisations in running their businesses.

The OECD Principles of Corporate Governance, first published in 1999, have been widely adopted as a benchmark both in OECD countries and elsewhere. They are used as one of 12 key standards by the Financial Stability Forum for ensuring international financial stability and by the World Bank in its work to improve corporate governance in emerging markets.(Saidi, 2008)

In 2002, OECD governments called for a review of the Principles to take account of developments in the corporate sector. The revised text is the product of a consultation process involving representatives of both OECD and non-OECD governments as well as of businesses and professional bodies, trade unions, civil society organisations and international standard-setting bodies. The OECD began a review of the principles in 2003 considering the recent changes and developments and after an extensive review the process led to adopt revised and reviewed OECD principles of corporate governance in April, 2004. The revision principles not only reflect the experience of OECD countries but also the emerging and developing economics. The revised principles are non-binding in nature and it lays up to the governments and market participants to decide for their own framework. It also confirmed the adaptability of the principles as a reference in varying legal, economic and cultural contexts. "Corporate governance is the system by which business corporations are directed and controlled . The corporate governance specifies the distribution of rights and responsibilities among different participants in the corporation, such as the board, managers, shareholders and other stakeholders, and spell out the rules and procedures for making decisions on corporate affairs. By doing this, it also provides the structures through which the company objectives are set, and the means of attaining those objectives and monitoring performance". The following are the main areas of the OECD principles and its annotation:(Abu-Tapanjeh, 2009)

Principle 1: *Ensuring the basis for an effective corporate governance framework.*

Annotation: The corporate governance framework

should promote transparent and efficient markets, be consistent with the rule of law and clearly articulate the division of responsibilities among different supervisory, regulatory and enforcement authorities.

Principle 2: *The right of shareholders and key ownership functions.*

Annotation: The corporate governance framework should protect and facilitate the exercise of shareholders' rights.

Principle 3: *The equitable treatment of shareholders.*

Annotation: The corporate governance framework should ensure the equitable treatment of all shareholders, including minority and foreign shareholders. All shareholders should have the opportunities to obtain effective redress for violation of their rights.

Principle 4: *The role of stakeholders in corporate governance.*

Annotation: The corporate governance framework should recognize the rights of stakeholders established by lawor through mutual agreements and encourage active co-operation between corporations and stakeholders in creating wealth, jobs, and the sustainability of financially sound enterprises.

Principle 5: *Disclosure and transparency.*

Annotation: The corporate governance framework should ensure that timely and accurate disclosure is made on all material matters regarding the corporation, including the financial situation, performance, ownership, and governance of the company.

Principle 6: *The responsibilities of the board.*

Annotation: The corporate governance framework should ensure the strategic guidance of the company, the effective monitoring of management by the board, and board's accountability to the company and the shareholders.

The main theme of the above principle lies in four basic principles. Firstly, the mechanism of business ethics, secondly the mechanism of decision making, thirdly in adequate disclosure and transparency and lastly the mechanism of book keeping and final accounts. These OECD principles are so sound that even the non-members of OECD are implementing and adopting. The soundness of these principles has been proved by its adoption all over the world the next section will discuss the Islamic view of corporate government from the Islamic perspective.

Researchers have defined corporate governance in a variety of ways, and the most widely cited definitions follow. The OECD defines CG as "a set of relationships between a company's management, its board, its shareholders and other stakeholders. Corporate Governance *also provides the structure through which the objectives of the company are set,* and the means of attaining those objectives and monitoring performance are determined".

This definition provides important attributes of CG and emphasizes transparency. However, it does not directly deal with the intrinsic issue of the business objectives that should guide the distribution of rights and responsibilities within the corporation. Indeed, the objectives of a corporation's founders', whether these be the increase of shareholders' value or the pursuit of stakeholders' interest, can be expected to affect such a distribution and shape the institutional structure and systems. In particular,the distribution of rights and responsibilities among shareholders and other stakeholders would be driven by the interests of whoever establishes the corporation and subsequently controls it.

The revised Principles emphasise the importance of a regulatory framework in corporate governance that promotes efficient markets, facilitates effective enforcement and clearly defines the responsibilities between different supervisory, regulatory and enforcement authorities. They also emphasise the need to ensure transparent lines of management responsibility within companies so as to make boards and management truly accountable. Other issues addressed by the revised Principles include:[1](OECD,

[1] See : OECD Principles of Corporate Governance. Available at:

2004)

Institutional investors

- They should disclose their corporate governance policies, how they decide on the use of their voting rights and how they manage conflicts of interest that may compromise their voting;
- Restrictions on consultations between shareholders about their voting intentions should be eased to reduce the cost of informed ownership.

Shareholder rights

- The rights of investors must be strengthened. Shareholders should be able to remove board members and participate effectively in the

---

- http://acts.oecd.org/Instruments/ShowInstrumentView.aspx?InstrumentID=151&InstrumentPID=147&Lang=en&Book=
- http://www.valuebasedmanagement.net/organizations_oecd.html
- http://www.valuebasedmanagement.net/articles_oecd_corporate_governance_principles_2004.html (visit 17/6/2014)

nomination and election processes;

- They should be able to make their views known about executive and board remuneration policy and any equity component should be subject to their approval.

Conflicts of interest and auditor responsibility

- A new principle calls for rating agencies and analysts to avoid conflicts of interest which could compromise their advice;
- The duties of the auditor must be strengthened and include accountability to shareholders and a duty to the company to exercise due professional care when conducting an audit;
- Auditors should be wholly independent and not be compromised by other relations with the company.

Stakeholder rights and whistle-blower protection

- The Principles make reference to the rights of

stakeholders, whether established by law or through mutual agreements.

- A new principle advocates protection for whistleblowers, including institutions through which their complaints or allegations can be addressed and provides for confidential access to a board member.

Board responsibilities

- The duties and responsibilities of the board have been clarified as fiduciary in nature, particularly important where company groups are concerned;
- The principle covering board independence and objectivity has been extended to avoid conflicts of interest and to cover situations characterised by block and controlling shareholders, as well as the board's responsibility for oversight of internal control systems covering financial reporting.

A concept of corporate governance from Islamic perspective does not differ much with the conventional definition as it refers to a system by which companies are directed and controlled with a purpose to meet the corporation's objective by protecting all the stakeholders' interest and right. Uniquely, in the context of corporate governance within the Islamic paradigm it presents distinct characteristics and features in comparison with the conventional system as it refers as a special case of a broader decision-making theory that uses the premise of Islamic socio- scientific epistemology which is premised on the divine oneness of God . A definition by the finance committee on corporate governance in Malaysia in the report on corporate governance stated that:

Corporate governance is the process and structure used to direct and manage the business and affairs of the company towards enhancing business prosperity and corporate accountability with the ultimate objective of realizing long term shareholder value, whilst taking account the interests of other stakeholders.

This indicates that corporate governance is not only applied to the shareholders but the other stakeholders as well.

Corporate governance in Islamic finance necessitates Islamic financial institutions abiding by a set of rules called the Islamic law or Shari'ah. The Shari'ah governs the bank's operations and transactions in accordance with Islamic principles derived from the Quran and Hadith.

Regulatory and corporate governance (CG) framework for IFIs

Regulatory and corporate governance (CG) framework of banks

I National CG framework

- Banking sector specific laws/codes/guidelines
- Stock exchanges listing rules and regulations
- Listed companies regulatory authorities laws, rules and regulations

II Islamic finance and *Shariah* specific codes and standards

- IFSB guiding principles on corporate governance for institutions offering Islamic financial services 2006[1]
- Accounting and auditing organisation for Islamic financial institutions (AAOIFI) accounting, auditing and governance standards (for Islamic financial institutions)[2]
- Islamic Financial Services Board (IFSB) published standards including guidance on key elements in the supervisory review process of institutions offering Islamic financial services (excluding Islamic insurance [*takaful*] institutions and Islamic mutual funds)

III International standards and codes

- The OECD principles of corporate governance[3]
- Guidance by the Basel committee on banking supervision on enhancing corporate governance for banking organisations 2006[4]

[1] http://www.ifsb.org/index.php?ch=4&pg=140
[2] www.aaoifi.com
[3] http://www.oecd.org/document/49/0,2340,en_2649_34813_31530865_1_1_1_1,00.html
[4] http://www.bis.org/publ/bcbs122.htm

Source: (Saidi, 2008)

The above **framework** suggests the build-up of a corporate governance framework for IFIs. To ensure that a national or sector specific CG framework is consistent with international best practice, the framework should incorporate the OECD pr and the BIS Guidelines.

1. Shari'ah Governance in Islamic Finance

Islamic financial institutions have the duty to ensure the compliance with Shari'ah principles in all aspects of their products, instruments, operations, practices and management which will be achieved by the establishment of a proper Shari'ah governance framework. Thus Shari'ah supervision plays an essential role in the governance of Islamic financial institution and forms part of the principal component of the Shari'ah governance framework. One of the roles of the Shari'ah supervisory board is to advise the Islamic financial instructions on Shari'ah matters to ensure conformity with Shari'ah rule in its operations at all time, endorsing and validating relevant documentations pertaining to the products and services of the Islamic financial institutions. The ideal role of Shari'ah supervision involve ex ante and ex post aspects of Shari'ah governance and these include Shari'ah pronouncement, supervision and review. In this aspect, the Sharia governance framework in Malaysia is based on the centralized model as compared to the decentralized being practiced in the GCC countries. The centralized model is formed on the basis that the Central Bank itself has its own Shari'ah supervisory board called the Shari'ah Advisory Board by virtue of section 51 of the Central Bank of Malaysia Act 2009 and all Islamic financial institutions are required to form their own Shari'ah committee which must comply with the rules set by the Shari'ah Advisory Board of the Central Bank. The importance of Shari'ah supervision is derived from five different resources namely religious, social, economic, legal and governance. The religious position is derived from the ability of Shari'ah scholars in understanding and interpreting Shari'ah principles to others. The social power of the Shari'ah supervision provides confidence to the stakeholders about the legitimacy of the transactions and activities of the Islamic financial institutions. The economic power of the Shari'ah supervision can be seen from the fact that the profitability of an Islamic financial institution is dependent on the performance of Shari'ah scholars. As far as legal power is concerned it is derived from a variety of sources including regulators of the respective countries. The hierarchical position of Shari'ah supervision under the shareholders of the Islamic

financial institutions emphasizes it supremacy over other governance organs thus giving them authority to set their internal policy including task, responsibilities and relations with other governance organs in the Islamic financial institutions.(Hasan, 2009, 2010, 2011)

The Shari'ah governance which refers to all the elements about the active role of the Shari'ah board and compliance with Shari'ah is fundamental to Islamic banks in particular and the implementation of Shari'ah governance is encouraged by international institutions of regulations like Accounting and Auditing Organization for Islamic Financial Institution (AAOIFI) and Islamic Financial Services Board Shari'ah board monitoring.

The SSB plays very important role in ensuring good Shari'ah governance. The role of the SSB is to include advising board of directors on Shari'ah matters to ensure that the operations comply with Shari'ah principles at all time, endorsing and validating relevant documentations pertaining to the products and services, as well as the internal policies and manuals and marketing advertisements.

Dynamic and good Shari'ah governance is the very essence in the development of Islamic banking and finance sector in Malaysia. Good Shari'ah governance guarantees the dynamicity of Islamic financial growth.

The interest of stakeholders may extend beyond the financial interest to ethical, religious or other values when requiring good corporate governance. In Islamic banks shareholders and Islamic scholars requires the operation of services offered to be under Shari'ah law otherwise it will be subject to process in no permission. Therefore, corporate governance through Shari'ah operation is essential.

Each Islamic bank or financial institution has in-house religious advisers, collectively known as SSB, as part of the internal governance structure of the institution, in some countries, authorities have created oversight arrangement, such as Shari'ah board in Islamic banking departments within supervisory agencies. These usually operate in connection with private independent market agents familiar with Islamic finance.

SSB prerogatives lie in five main areas: certification of permissible financial instruments though fatwas (*ex ante Shari'ah* audit), verification of transactions' compliance with issued fatwa (*ex post Shari'ah* audit) the calculation and payment of Zakat, disposal of non Shari'ahpayment compliant earning, advise to the distribution of income or expenses among the bank shareholders and investment account holders. Each SBB issues a report to certify the Shari'ah compliance of all financial transactions. In addition to SSB, most Islamic financial institutions have established another internal Shari'ah Review structure namely Shari'ah Review units. These units are independent of other departments or are an integral part of the internal audit and control department.

In recent years, the Islamic Financial Services Board (IFSB) has developed three Guiding Principles to help strengthen governance structures and processes in various segments of the Islamic financial services industry (IFSI) in line with its mandate to promote soundness and stability of the Islamic financial system.It was noted that in all three projects, concerns over the roles and functions of the *Shari`ah* boards, which constitute part of the broader governance system, have been a recurring theme. This is crucial, considering that compliance with *Shari`ah* rules and principles is the *raison d'être* of the IFSI. In fact, other IFSB standards – such as those on risk management, capital adequacy and supervisory review process – also contain requirements and recommendations aimed at ensuring that an appropriate *Shari`ah* governance system is in place.

Consequently, the IFSB Council, during its ninth meeting in Jeddah, approved the preparation of a set of Guiding Principles on the *Shari`ah* governance system, which is expected to:(Hasan, 2009, 2010, 2011)

(a) complement other prudential standards issued by the IFSB by highlighting in more detail to the supervisory authorities in particular, and the industry's other stakeholders in general, the components of a sound *Shari`ah* governance system, especially with regard to the competence, independence, confidentiality and consistency of *Shari`ah* boards;

(b) facilitate better understanding of *Shari`ah* governance issues and how stakeholders should satisfy themselves that an appropriate and effective *Shari`ah* governance system is in place;

(c) provide an enhanced degree of transparency in terms of issuance, and the audit/review process for compliance with *Shari`ah* rulings; and

(d) provide greater harmonization of the *Shari`ah* governance structures and procedures across jurisdictions, especially since there are increasing numbers of IIFS with cross-border operations.

The term "Shari'ah Governance System", despite being commonly used within the IFSI to refer to structures and processes adopted by stakeholders in the IFSI (from financial regulators to market players) to ensure compliance with Shari'ah rules and principles, has not been properly defined in any of the existing standards. In the interests of clarity, this document shall adopt the following definition of "*Shari'ah* Governance System" and the other key terminology:

"*Shari'ah* Governance System" refers to the set of institutional and organizational arrangements through which an IIFS ensures that there is effective independent oversight of *Shari'ah* compliance over each of the following structures and processes:(Hasan, 2009, 2010, 2011)

(a) *Issuance of relevant Shari'ah pronouncements/resolutions*

"*Shari'ah* pronouncements/resolutions" refers to a juristic opinion on any matter pertaining to *Shari`ah* issues in Islamic finance, given by the appropriately mandated *Shari`ah* board. In jurisdictions where there is a central authority such as the national *Shari`ah* board or *Fatwa* Council, that central authority has the power to issue such pronouncements/resolutions, resulting in the *Shari`ah* board at the IIFS usually focusing only on ensuring that the IIFS is compliant with the pronouncements/resolutions issued by the central authority. Once it is decided that a *Shari`ah* pronouncement/resolution should actually be implemented, it becomes a "*Shari`ah* ruling" (*hukm al-Shar'i*) with full legal effect that binds the IIFS.A *Shari`ah* pronouncement/resolution shall be issued only through appropriate due processes, which, amongst others, should involve rigorous deliberation among members of the *Shari`ah* board over any proposed *Shari`ah*-compliant products or transactions that require a *Shari'ah* endorsement, as well as detailed scrutiny of the legal contracts and other documents relevant to the products or transactions.

(b) *Dissemination of information on such Shari'ah pronouncements/resolutions to the operative personnel of the IIFS who monitor the day-to-day compliance with the Shari'ah pronouncements/resolutions vis-à-vis every level of operations and each transaction* Such a task would normally be undertaken by a designated "internal *Shari`ah* compliance unit/department (ISCU)", or at least a *Shari`ah* compliance officer who is part of the IIFS's compliance team. The IIFS shall equip the ISCU with the appropriate compliance- monitoring skills and relevant knowledge of the *shari'a* – for example, by assembling a team of staff with the two different skill-sets. The IIFS should also ensure that the ISCU is separate and independent from the business units and departments.

(c) *An internal Shari`ah compliance review/ audit for verifying that Shari`ah compliance has been satisfied,during which any incident of non-compliance will be recorded and reported, and as far as possible, addressed and rectified* IFSB-3 sets out that *Shari`ah* pronouncements/ resolutions issued by the *Shari`ah* boards should be strictly adhered to. The internal *Shari`ah* review would therefore be assigned to someone adequately trained in *Shari`ah* compliance review/audit, so that he or she would have a competent grasp of the process.

While the ISCU is part of the IIFS's compliance team,the internal *Shari`ah* review/audit unit/department (ISRU) may be established to function in a similar manncr to thc IIFS's intcrnal audit team. The major difference is that while the internal auditor will usually report to the Audit Committee, the ISRU shall report to the *Shari`ah* board.

Where appropriate, the internal *Shari`ah* review/audit reports shall require or recommend the management of the IIFS to address and rectify any issues of *Shari`ah* compliance.

(d) *An annual Shari`ah compliance review/audit for verifying that the internal Shari`ah compliance review/audit has been appropriately carried out and its findings have been duly noted by the Shari`ah board* The *Shari`ah* board who issued the *Shari`ah* pronouncements/resolutions can take charge of this process, having received feedback and reports from the ISRU. Alternatively, this task may be assigned to an appropriately competent external auditor or external *Shari'ah* firm.

The *Shari'ah* board or *Shari'ah* advisory firm that carries out the *Shari'ah* compliance review/audit shall produce reports, indicating whether the IIFS has complied with *Shari'ah* requirements throughout the financial year.

Where appropriate and if deemed necessary, there could be two sets of reports produced: a general statement of compliance that should be included in the annual report of the IIFS; and a more detailed account of compliance work undertaken addressed specifically to the supervisory authorities.

2. *Shari'ah* Governance Model from Regulatory Perspective

Shari'ah governance system as defined by The IFSB Guiding Principles on *Sharia* Governance System in Institutions Offering Islamic Financial Services (IFSB-10) refers to a set of institutional and organizational arrangements to oversee *Shari'ah* compliance aspects in Islamic Financial Institutions (IFIs).

In this regard, majority of IFIs have established their own *Shari'ah* board and some of them even have set up a dedicated internal *Shari'ah* review unit or department to support *Shari'ah* board in performing its function. This indicates a positive development on the aspect of *Shari'ah* governance system in IFIs. Looking at the different framework and style of *Shari'ah* governance in various legal environment and diverse banking models.

privilege which prevents them from being taken a legal action by the Islamic financial institution, if it can be proven that such duties was conducted in good faith.

Corporate governance has gained great prominence over the last three decades even in the conventional financial system because of continued financial instability. It would be of even greater importance in the Islamic system because of the additional risk to which the depositors would get exposed when the banks really start moving into the risk-sharing modes. This poses an important challenge before Islamic banks to improve all crucial aspects of corporate governance. The challenge will become more serious as these institutions expand and their problems become more complex. This challenge could be successfully met if the Board of Directors and Senior Management become more effective in the performance of their responsibilities.(Chapra & Ahmed, 2002)

Effective corporate governance in banks as well as the firms that use bank funds is one of the most important pillars of the new environment that needs to be created to replace the old socio-economic environment that no longer exists. Unfortunately, however, corporate governance is considered to be generally weak in the corporations of most developing countries. This is because all the institutions that play a crucial role in disciplining markets and ensuring efficiency and integrity are not well-developed in these countries. Information asymmetries are more severe, market participants less experienced, and regulations, even if they exist, do not get enforced effectively and impartially because of political corruption and the general weakness of judicial systems. Disclosures are also not adequate and accounting practices are not well developed. Consequently, these corporations suffer from inefficiencies and inequities that adversely affect all stakeholders. The adverse effects of ineffective corporate governance can be more serious in the case of financial institutions because the number of their stakeholders is much larger and the systemic risks are much greater. There is no reason to assume that, even though the Islamic financial institutions have done fairly well so far, they have necessarily been able to escape the trappings of the prevailing weak corporate governance in developing countries. It should be possible to improve their performance considerably and to serve the interests of all stakeholders much better by making corporate governance more effective in these institutions. Therefore, the strong rationale for greater reliance on equity in an Islamic economy intensifies the need for adoption of all those measures that would not only help improve the functioning of the financial system but also safeguard the interests of all stakeholders. (Chapra & Ahmed, 2002)

Without effective corporate governance, it may not be possible to strengthen Islamic banks and to enable them to expand rapidly and perform their role effectively. This need will become more and more serious as the institutions expand and their problems become more complex – problems which will erode their ability in the long-run to meet successfully the challenges that they face. It is, therefore, not possible to avoid the taking of all those measures that would help improve the functioning of these institutions.

For this purpose, it is important to sharpen the tools of corporate governance, the most important of which are: internal controls, risk management, transparency, loan accounting and disclosure, *Shari'ah* clearance and audit, external audit, and prudential regulation and supervision. Total reliance on these would, however, not be sufficient. Moral commitment on the part of all market operators is indispensable. Without such commitment, market operators will find different ways of violating the law without getting detected and punished. This will create the need for more and more legal checks and controls, which will raise transactions costs to an unbearably high level. Making them truly accountable before shareholders and depositors by the adoption of measures discussed in this paper should also be of great help. What is also needed is the establishment of a number of shared institutions as discussed above. Without such institutions even banks with the best corporate governance may not be able to avoid crises.

However, corporate governance is generally weak in all countries and particularly so in developing countries, in which category nearly all Muslim countries fall at present. This is because all the institutions that play a crucial role in disciplining markets and ensuring efficiency and integrity are not well-developed in these countries. Information asymmetries are more severe, market participants less experienced, and regulations, even if they exist, do not always get enforced effectively and impartially because of political corruption and the general weakness of judicial systems. Disclosures are also not adequate and accounting practices are not well developed. The adverse effects of ineffective corporate governance can be more serious in the case of financial institutions because their leverage is much higher, the number of their stakeholders is more extensive, and the systemic risks of their failure are far more serious. There is no reason to assume that, even though the Islamic financial institutions have done fairly well so far, they have necessarily been able to escape the trappings of the prevailing weak corporate governance in developing countries. It is, therefore, not possible to avoid the taking of all those measures that would help improve the functioning of these institutions. The role of the Board of Directors and Senior Management is of crucial importance in this respect. It is gratifying to note that almost all Muslim countries are presently in the process of implementing the BCBS guidelines.(Hasan, 2011)

A. The Board of Directors

The Board of Directors cannot, however, play this role

effectively if its members do not have a high degree of moral integrity as well as professional competence in banking business. They must be adequately aware of the risks and complexities involved in the banking business. In an Islamic system, they must have the additional qualification of being well-versed in the *Shari'ah* and its objectives and in particular the rationale behind the prohibition of interest. They should ensure adequate transparency in keeping with the standards laid down by the BCBS, the IFSB and the supervisory authority of their own country through a smooth flow of relevant information to directors, senior Management, auditors, supervisors, shareholders, depositors and the public according to the needs of each with a view to ensure a proper check on the affairs of the bank. They must establish a strong internal control system, proper accounting procedures, effective internal and external audit, efficient risk management, and all necessary checks and balances, rules, regulations and procedures.(Hasan, 2011)

Experience has shown that directors do not necessarily perform their roles effectively. There are a number of reasons for this. One of these is that the Board members may not necessarily have the professional competence and the moral integrity that are needed to manage the bank efficiently. Another reason is that Board members are not always genuinely elected by shareholders and are not necessarily accountable before them. Elections do not take place regularly at defined intervals and, even if they do, evidence indicates that shareholders are not actively involved in the election or removal of directors. This enables board members to perpetuate themselves and it is generally difficult to dislodge them except through takeovers. These are, however, expensive and potentially disruptive and, may not, therefore, be a possible remedy except in extreme cases. To correct this situation, it is necessary to have a transparent procedure for elections and to adopt measures that would enable minority shareholders and investment depositors to have a say in Board decisions. It is also necessary to enable shareholders to remove

Board members in the event of their performance falling far short of what they expect. It is, therefore, imperative to institute reforms in election procedures as well as proxy rules to enable shareholders to elect competent and conscientious persons to the Board of Directors and to prevent them from perpetuating themselves in spite of their poor performance.

It is also necessary to develop a legal and regulatory infrastructure to protect the rights of not only minority shareholders but also depositors (both being outsiders). In a number of countries companies are allowed to ask registered shareholders, who are unable to attend general meetings, to transfer their votes to the Board of Directors. This further strengthens the hands of the Board and enables it to control decisions at shareholder meetings. Since the transfer of voting rights often leads to far-reaching consequences, which may not always be in the interest of all stakeholders, it would be desirable to transfer voting rights to shareholder associations, if they exist. If such associations do not exist, then voting rights may be transferred to supervisory authorities or to specialized chartered firms established in the private sector to protect the interest of stakeholders against a fee as discussed later. All three of these institutions would perhaps be better qualified to protect the interests of stakeholders.(Hasan, 2010)

It would also be helpful if there are an adequate number of non-executive directors on the Board. Empirical evidence in the conventional system indicates that non-executive directors influence positively a Board's capabilities to evaluate and discipline managers. This is perhaps because such directors do not have any management responsibility and may not, therefore, have a vested interest in protecting the management. They may, therefore, be expected to attach greater weight to the interests of minority shareholders and depositors and, thereby, help inject equity into the company. If they do not come up to this expectation, they would hurt their own reputation in the directors' labour market. Removal of the Chief Executive Officer (CEO) caused by poor performance is more likely in outsider dominated Boards than in insider dominated ones. However, here too there are problems. If the non-executive directors have not been elected by shareholders but rather handpicked by the dominant shareholder or the CEO, they would owe their careers to him and would, therefore, 'lack the information and incentives required to provide consistent effective corporate governance'. There will, thus, be conflict of interest, which will create a lack of willingness on their part to discipline senior management. Moreover, Board meetings may not be frequent and non-executive directors may not, therefore, be able to monitor the activities of the company effectively and ensure correction, particularly if overt criticism of management policies in board meetings is considered to be rude Since Islamic banks are generally small compared with their conventional counterparts even in Muslim countries, leave alone the rest of the world, the amount of capital held by them is also very small. This enables concentration of shares in the hands of a few executive directors. The number of non-executive directors who can serve as a check on the executive directors is also accordingly small. Since the small size as well as the concentration of shareholdings carries the potential of leading to undesired consequences for protecting the interests of all stakeholders, it is desirable to enlarge the size of banks and to institute legal reforms with the objective of reducing concentration, diversifying risks, and increasing the ability of these banks to absorb losses.

It would also be desirable to introduce some other reforms to make the Board of Directors more effective in its functions. One of these, which needs to be considered seriously, is to relate the remuneration of Board members to their performance in the same way as required in *mudaraba* contracts. The directors in their capacity as *mudaribs* (managing entrepreneurs) should be compensated for only their actual expenses and not be entitled to a fixed management fee or remuneration as they do in modern corporations. Their remuneration should be a certain percent of the profit earned by the bank, if the bank makes a profit. This must be in addition to their normal share in profit like other shareholders on the basis of their shareholdings. The percentage share of profits to be allocated to the directors for their management services must be clearly specified in the Articles of Agreement so that it is well-known to the shareholders. If the corporation makes a profit, the directors get the specified percent of profit for their services. But if the corporation makes a loss, the directors do not, like the *mudarib,* get a 'fee' for their management services, and should share in the losses in proportion to their stockholdings. The directors would thus get a reward for their services only if they have contributed to profits – the higher the profit, the greater their reward. This should prove to be an incentive to them for better performance.(Hasan, 2011)

B. Senior management

While the Board of Directors refers to persons who are generally not only shareholders themselves but also participate in the governance of the bank, senior management refers to the CEO and other senior members of the staff who perform management functions but are not necessarily shareholders. Modern corporations are in general not managed by their owners (shareholders). Instead, professional managers are hired to run the business. They are 'fiduciaries'.[1] This creates the principal/agent problem and leads to a conflict of interests. It is, therefore, necessary to impose restrictions on self-dealing, fraud, excessive compensation in different hidden forms, and other malpractices.

One of the most important constraints on management is that key positions should not be held by one person ('four eyes principle'). Since the CEO and the Chairman of the Board perform two distinct functions in the bank, it would be preferable to have two different persons holding these positions so that there is a clear division of responsibilities at the top of the bank to ensure independence and balance of power and authority. Neither the directors nor the management should be allowed to stay on the job if they are no longer competent or qualified to run the bank. As argued by Jensen and Ruback, poor managers who resist being replaced might be the costliest manifestation of the agency problem.(Hasan, 2011)

It is the responsibility of the Board of Directors and senior management to ensure proper internal controls, and effective management of all risks, including credit risk, liquidity risk, interest-rate risk, and operational risks. Even though the exposure of most Islamic banks to these risks seems to be relatively high, they have been able to manage them fairly well so far. Nevertheless, this may not necessarily continue in the future. It is, therefore, extremely important to cultivate an effective risk management culture in these banks to ensure their competitiveness and survival in a world full of uncertainties and crises. This cannot, however, be done without the active collaboration of Board of

Directors, senior management, the *Shari'ah* scholars, and bank supervisors.

C. Regulatory and Internal Frameworks

1. Proactive Approach and Integrated Corporate and Shari'ah Governance

In view of the numerous challenges faced by Islamic finance, it is recommended that the industry needs a regulatory-based approach framework as explained before. As a prerequisite, *Shari'ah* governance must be part of the concerns of regulators and policymakers. The regulators should proactively monitor the implementation of *Shari'ah* governance and learn from the experience of other jurisdictions in nurturing the *Shari'ah* governance framework. The principle of 'one-size-fits-all' *Shari'ah* governance is not appropriate as the market and local legal environments are different from one place to another. In designing the *Shari'ah* governance framework, it is a matter of necessity to have an integrated corporate and *Shari'ah* governance framework. These two things must not be segregated as they complement each other. In this aspect, the principles or guidelines on corporate governance must take into account the element of *Shari'ah* governance when it involves institutions offering Islamic financial services. This is important because the stakeholder-oriented model of governance in IFIs requires them to protect the rights and interests of all stakeholders.(Hasan, 2011)

2. Supervision and Enforcement

The regulators should have a comprehensive framework in the aspects of supervision and enforcement and these include written guidelines on supervision for supervisors, directives for IFIs issued by supervisors, sufficient resources with adequate knowledge on *Shari'ah* governance-related matters and full authority to carry out the enforcement functions. The supervisors should provide guidelines and make sure that they evaluate the internal policies and procedures as well as the implementation of these procedures. It is also important for the supervisors to consistently inspect the IFIs by having a proper framework in place which allows them to make an assessment of IFIs' Shari'ah governance policies and tools to redress any deficiencies.

3. Dispute Settlement

It would be an ideal development if the regulators initiated a special bench for Islamic finance cases as part of the court's structure. In this special bench, the court may appoint judges who are knowledgeable in Islamic finance or the regulators may allocate a certain amount of funds to provide training for those judges. On top of that, a reliable Shari'ah litigation system must also be in place. It is understood that in a secular legal environment, such as in the UK, the above arrangement is slightly difficult to implement. Therefore, it is important for the regulators in the secular legal environment to consider a court referral to a shari'a board or a *Shari'ah* expert to determine cases involving *Shari'ah* issues. Alternatively, a special tribunal for Islamic finance cases may be established to handle disputes involving IFIs in this kind of jurisdiction. The policymakers should also take into account other legal avenues for dispute settlement, such as arbitration and mediation. At this point in time, there are several institutions for international dispute resolution, such as the Dubai Centre for Arbitration and Conciliation, the GCC Commercial Arbitration Centre, the Bahrain Centre for International Commercial Arbitration Centre, the International Chamber of Commerce's International Court of Arbitration, the London Court of International Arbitration, the Kuwait Centre for Commercial Arbitration, the Kuala Lumpur Arbitration Centre and others. In view of these numerous arbitration centers, it is recommended that there should be one specific institution that offers alternative dispute resolutions and settlement for Islamic finance cases. Alternatively, the existing arbitration centers should develop and enhance their expertise and capabilities in Islamic finance in terms of resources, frameworks, procedures and facilities. At this point, these institutions for arbitration must prepare to facilitate themselves with necessary facilities and resources to address the need for dispute settlement involving Islamic finance cases.(Hasan, 2010)

In order to ensure the effectiveness of the arbitration, the decision or solution of the arbitration should be made binding and conclusive. The legally binding effect in arbitration is crucial for the purpose of ensuring credibility and confidence in any solution made in the arbitration. In spite of that, it is also important for the regulators to encourage arbitration as an alternative legal avenue for dispute settlement and to issue policies and procedures that clearly acknowledge Islamic law as the main source of law as a basis for decision-making.

4. Well-conceived By-laws and Internal Policies

Well-conceived by-laws and internal policies are prerequisites of effective Shari'ah governance. Realizing this, the IFIs should have appropriate by-laws and policies as guidelines for their internal use in terms of meeting procedures, decision-making, preparing reports and dissemination of information, records and reviews. At this point, the IFSB-10 and the AAOIFI governance standards may be the basis for such by-laws, with some modifications that would be appropriate to be implemented within the local market and regulatory environment.

D. Attributes of the Shari'ah Board on Independence

Following are the attributes of being Shari'ah board independence: (Hasan, 2009, 2010, 2011)

1. Method of Appointment

There are significant differences in the method of appointment of the Shari'ah board between IFIs. It is also found that numerous IFIs did not comply with the AAOIFI governance standards in that their appointments are made by the BOD and not the shareholders. In view of the actual market practice and more practical tools for ensuring independence, There are other mechanisms that would be appropriate to achieve such an objective. Firstly, the appointment must be made either by the BOD or the shareholders. Secondly, the appointment must be subject to the approval of the regulatory authorities. Thirdly, the appointment must not be permanent but rather contractual subject to renewal. Fourthly, the termination and dismissal must also be subject to the approval of the regulatory authorities.(Hasan, 2011)

2. Code of Conduct

The majority of IFIs do not have a code of ethics for Shari'ah board. The existing practices seem to presume that Shari'ah board members are bound by Islamic ethical principles. In view of the need to have a certain and precise code of ethics specific and exclusive to the Shari'ah board, the regulatory authorities as well as the IFIs may prescribe certain acceptable behavior for Shari'ah board members. It is incumbent upon the IFIs to initiate and develop an internal code of conduct for the Shari'ah board. This code of ethics should be enforceable and there must be a mechanism within the organizational structure to ensure its strict implementation. Breach of this code of ethics may incur disciplinary action such as suspension, termination or other kinds of sanctions.

3. Professional Body

There is no professional body specifically established to set a standard practice for the Shari'ah board as is the case for other professionals such as lawyers, accountants, medical practitioners and engineers. The establishment of a professional body to set the qualifications of the Shari'ah board, to introduce a standard code of conduct, to develop a training program and to enhance the professionalism of the Shari'ah board is consider necessary at this point in time. At the moment, different bodies attempt to provide qualification programs for Shari'ah boards, such as the AAOIFI Certified Shari'ah Adviser and Auditor, the Scholar Development Program initiated by the IFC Islamic finance council and the SII and the IBFIM Shari'ah Scholars Introduction Program, but it was found that such qualifications have not been accepted universally. The study strongly recommends the establishment of The Association of *Shari'ah* Advisors at the national and international levels.235 With this association, the quality of the Shari'ah board can then also be rated by an independent agency similar to a credit-rating agency.

4. Remuneration Policy

There are significant differences in the remuneration of different Shari'ah boards. The absence of any policy limitation or guidelines on the Shari'ah board's remuneration may lead to unhealthy practices. The top ten Shari'ah scholars who dominated the board positions in IFIs around the world earn a very lucrative and significant amount of remuneration. It was found that a chairman of a Shari'ah board could earn USD50,000 to USD100,000 per board and a top scholar could even gain up to USD250,000 on a typical capital markets deal. This study further estimates that the top five Shari'ah scholars may earn up to a million dollars per year for servicing more than a hundred board and chairman positions around the world. While there is no standard benchmark or scale fee for Shari'ah advisors, the regulators as well as the IFIs should establish a specific policy for the remuneration of Shari'ah board members based on the appropriate scale fees. In the context of the internal policy of IFIs, the Shari'ah board scale fees should be approved by the shareholders and disclosed in the annual report.(Hasan, 2011)

5. Attributes of the Shari'ah Board on Confidentiality

There were Shari'ah scholars who have unintentionally or indirectly disclosed some confidential information, particularly those sitting on the boards of numerous IFIs. In addition, the survey results indicated that 29% of IFIs view that the Shari'ah board is not fully aware of the issue of confidentiality. Realizing this, the IFIs should have a proper mechanism to resolve this issue and this includes terms of reference in the letter of appointment, enforcement of the code of ethics and disciplinary proceedings for any misconduct by the Shari'ah board. In defining the scope of confidentiality, a reference may be made to section 52 of the IFSB-10. The IFSB-10 nevertheless does not provide guidelines for disciplinary proceedings in the event that Shari'ah board members breach confidentiality or disclose sensitive or confidential information. As such, the IFIs are recommended to have proper disciplinary proceedings, such as hearing procedures, and rules of evidence with an appropriate organizational structure.(Hasan, 2011)

Future directions

The further growth and development of the Islamic financial system will depend largely on the nature of innovations introduced in the market. The immediate need is to deploy human and financial resources to develop instruments to enhance liquidity;Develop secondary, money, and interbank markets; perform asset/liability and risk management; and introduce public finance instruments. The Islamic financial system can also offer alternatives at the microfinance level. Securitization is a step in the right direction but even this requires more sophistication. The scope of securitization —the process of unbundling and repackaging a financial asset to enhance its mar- ketability, negotiability, and liquidity—in Islamic financial markets is very promising, because current market operations are restricted by the dearth of liquidity-enhancing products; secondary markets lack depth and breadth; and, more important, instruments for asset/liability management are simply nonexistent. With the expansion of securitization, the customer base of Islamic financial systems will grow as institutional investors, who have access to broader maturity structures, are attracted to the market; The secondary market will develop; and asset/liability management will become a reality. Other strong candidates for securitization include real estate, leasing, and trade receivables because of the collateralized nature of their cash flows.

Microfinance is another candidate for the application of Islamic finance. Islamic finance promotes entrepreneurship and risk sharing, and its expansion to the poor could be an effective development tool. The social benefits are obvious, since the poor currently are often exploited by lenders charging usurious rates.

An Islamic financial system can play a vital role in the economic development of Islamic countries by mobilizing dormant savings that are being intentionally kept out of interest-based financial channels and by facilitating the development of capital markets. At the same time, the development of such systems would enable savers and borrowers to choose financial instruments compatible with their business needs, social values, and religious beliefs.(Elasrag, 9. April 2011; Iqbal, 1997)

GLOSSARY

Bay`	Sale or contract of sale.
Bay` al-`Inah	A contract involving the sale and buy-back transaction of assets by a seller. A seller sells an asset to a buyer on a cash basis and later buys it back on a deferred payment basis where the price is higher than the cash price. It can also be applied when a seller sells an asset to a buyer on a deferred basis and later buys it back on a cash basis, at a price which is lower than the deferred
Commodity *Murābahah*	A *Murābahah*-based purchase and sale transaction of *Sharī`ah*- compliant commodities, whereby the buyer purchases the commodities on a deferred payment basis and subsequently sells them to a third party on a cash payment basis.

Darūrah	Darūrah is an exigency in the event that if the necessary act is not done, then it shall lead to the destruction of five fundamental needs, namely religion, life, intelligence, progeny and property. The principle of *Darūrah* is only applicable in exceptional circumstances where the avoidance of the specific necessary act shall ruin the said fundamentals.
***Fatawa* (singular *Fatwa*)**	A juristic opinion or pronouncement of facts given by the *Sharī`ah* board, a *Mufti*, or a *Faqīh* on any matter pertinent to *Sharī`ah* issues, based on the appropriate methodology.
Gharar	Deceptive uncertainty where details concerning the sale contract are unknown or uncertain.
I`ādat Al Shirā'	Repurchase

Ijārah	An *Ijārah* contract is an agreement made by an institution offering Islamic financial services to lease to a customer an asset specified by the customer for an agreed period against specified instalments of lease rental. An *Ijārah* contract commences with a promise to lease that is binding on the part of the potential lessee prior to entering the *Ijārah* contract.
Istisnā`	An *Istisnā`* contract is an agreement to sell to a customer a non- existent asset, which is to be manufactured or built according to the buyer"s specifications and is to be delivered on a specified future date at a pre-determined selling price.
Kafālah	Guarantee
Kafālah bi al-Ujr	Charging fee for guarantee
Maslahah	Public interest
Maysir	Gambling
Mu`addal Ribh	Floating rate
Mu`addal Ribh	*Fixed rate*
Mubādalah	Swap
Mubādalah al-	Profit rate swaps

Muḍārabah	A *Muḍārabah* contract is an agreement between the capital provider and a skilled entrepreneur whereby the capital provider will contribute capital to an enterprise or activity, which is to be managed by the entrepreneur as the *Muḍārib*. Profits generated by that enterprise or activity are shared in accordance with the terms of the *Muḍārabah* agreement, whilst losses are to borne solely by the capital provider unless the losses are due to the *Muḍārib's* misconduct, negligence or breach of contracted terms.
Muḍārib	Labour provider
Murābahah	A *Murābahah* contract is an agreement whereby the institution offering Islamic financial services sells to a customer a specified kind of asset that is already in their possession at cost plus an agreed profit margin (selling price).

Mushārakah	A *Mushārakah* contract is an agreement between the institution offering Islamic financial services and a customer to contribute capital to an enterprise, whether existing or new, or to own a real estate or moveable asset, either on a temporary or permanent basis. Profits generated by that enterprise or real estate/asset are shared in accordance with the terms of the *Mushārakah* agreement, whilst losses are shared in proportion to each partner"s share of capital.
Muslim	A believer in or adherent of Islam.
Qarḍ / Qarḍ al-Hasan	A non-interest bearing loan intended to allow the borrower to use the loaned funds for a period with the understanding that the same amount of the loaned funds would be repaid at the end of the period.
Rahn	A contract to pledge a specified asset as security against a debt whereby the creditor (*Murtahin*) is entitled to hold custody of the asset. In the event of default by the debtor (*Rāhin*), the creditor may sell the asset.
ReTakāful	Islamic re-insurance
Riba	Usury
Sadaqah	Donation

Salam	A *Salam* contract is an agreement to purchase, at a pre-determined price, a specified kind of commodity not available with the seller, which is to be delivered on a specified future date in a specified quantity and quality. The institution offering Islamic financial services, as the buyer, makes full payment of the purchase price upon execution of a *Salam* contract. The commodity may or may not be traded over the counter or on an exchange.
Sharī`ah	Divine Islamic law that encompasses all aspects of human life as revealed in the *Qur'an* and the *Sunnah*.

***Sukūk* (singular *Sakk*)**	*Sukūk* (certificates) each of which represents the holder"s proportionate ownership in an undivided part of an underlying asset where the holder assumes all rights and obligations to such an asset.
Tabarru'	Grant of property by a person with complete legal capacity without any compensation. In the context of *Takāful* operations, *Tabarru'* is the amount of contribution to be relinquished by the *Takāful* participant as a donation for fulfilling the obligation of mutual help and to be used to pay claims submitted by eligible claimants.
Tahawwut	Hedging
Takāful	*Takāful* is derived from an Arabic word which means solidarity, whereby a group of participants agree among themselves to support one another jointly against a specified loss. In a *Takāful* arrangement, the participants contribute a sum of money as *Tabarru'* (donation) into a common fund, which will be used for the mutual assistance of the members against specified loss or damage.

Tawarruq	Purchasing an asset with deferred price, either on the basis of *Musawamah* (sale contract without the disclosure of the asset cost price and profit margin to the buyer) or *Murābahah*, then selling it to a third party to obtain cash.
Wa'd	A promise to perform certain action(s) in the future.
Wakālah	An agency contract where the customer (principal) appoints the institution offering Islamic financial services as an agent (*Wakīl*) to carry out business on their behalf.
***Waqf* (plural *Awqāf*)**	A property that produces income and that may have been deeded to benefit a community.
Zakat	Alms giving

LIST OF ABBREVIATIONS

AAOIFI Accounting and Auditing Organisation for Islamic Financial Institutions

ADB Asian Development Bank

ADR Advance-deposit ratio

ALA Alternative liquidity approaches

ALFI Association of the Luxembourg Fund Industry

ASRR Advances to Stable Resources Ratio

ATM Automated teller machine

BCBS Basel Committee on Banking Supervision

BCP Basel Core Principles for Effective Banking Supervision

BDL Banque du Liban

BIBF Bahrain Institute of Banking and Finance

BMI Broad Market Index

BNM Bank Negara Malaysia

BU Bottom-up

CAGR Compound annual growth rate

CAR Capital adequacy ratio

CBB Central Bank of Bahrain

CBRT Central Bank of the Republic of Turkey

CBUAE Central Bank of the United Arab Emirates

CDs Certificates of deposit

CEBS Committee of European Banking Supervisors

CFEB Consumer Financial Education Body

CGAP Consultative Group to Assist the Poor

CIB Credit Information Bureau

CMF Collateralised Murābahah Facility

CMT	Commodity Murābahah transactions
CPs	Core principles
CSR	Corporate social responsibility
D-SIBs	Domestic systemically important banks
DJIM	Dow Jones Islamic Market Indices
DOF	Department of Finance
EBA	European Banking Authority
ECAIS	External credit assessment institutions
ECB	European Central Bank
ED	Exposure Draft
EIBOR	Emirates Interbank Offer Rate
ELA	Emergency Liquidity Assistance
EMDEs	Emerging market and developing economies
Eurosif	European Sustainable Investment Forum
ESG	Environmental, social and corporate governance
ESRB	European Systemic Risk Board
ETFs	Exchange traded funds
EU	European Union
FCY	Foreign currency
FDR	Financing-to-deposit ratio
FIS	Facilitating of Standards
FSA	Financial Services Authority
FSAP	Financial Sector Assessment Programme
FSB	Financial Stability Board
FSL	Financial stability law

FX Foreign exchange

GATE Global Commodity Finance Ltd.

GCC Gulf Cooperation Council

GDP Gross domestic product

GLP Gross loan portfolio

GPRS General Packet Radio Service

G-SIBs Global systematically important banks

G-SIIs Global systemically important insurers

G-SIFIs Global systematically important financial institutions

HQLA High-quality liquid assets

IADI International Association of Deposit Insurers

IAHs Investment account holders

IAIS International Association of Insurance Supervisors

IASB International Accounting Standards Board

IBB Islamic Bank of Britain

IBIs Islamic banks and Islamic banking windows

ICs Investment Companies

ICAAP Internal capital adequacy assessment process

ICMM Islamic Capital and Money Market

ICP Insurance Core Principles, Standards, Guidance and Assessment Methodology

IDB Islamic Development Bank

IFRS International Financial Reporting Standards

IFSB Islamic Financial Services Board

IFSI Islamic financial services industry

IIBOR Islamic Interbank Offered Rate

IIFM	International Islamic Financial Market
IIFS	Institutions offering Islamic financial services
IILM	International Islamic Liquidity Management Corporation
IIMM	Islamic Interbank Money Market
ILO	International Labour Organization
IMF	International Monetary Fund
INCEIF	International Centre for Education in Islamic Finance
IOSCO	International Organization of Securities Commissions
IRR	Investment risk reserve
IRTI	Islamic Research and Training Institute
ISDA	International Swaps and Derivatives Association, Inc.
ISLI	Islamic Sukūk Liquidity Instrument
LCR	Liquidity Coverage Ratio
LCY	Local currency
LIBOR	London Interbank Offer Rate
LOLR	Lender of last resort
MDIC	Malaysia Deposit Insurance Corporation
MENA	Middle East and North Africa
MFBs	Microfinance Banks
MFIs	Microfinance Institutions
NGOs	Non-governmental organisations
NPF	Non-performing financing
NPLs	Non-performing loans
NSFR	Net Stable Funding Ratio
ODTIs	Other deposit taking institutions

OECD	Organisation for Economic Co-operation and Development
OIC	Organization of Islamic Conferences
OMOs	Open market operations
OTC	Over-the-counter
PIF	Participants" Investment Fund
PMN	Pakistan Microfinance Network
POS	Point-of-sale
PRF	Participants" Risk Fund
PRI	Principles for Responsible Investment
PSE	Public sector entities
PSIA	Profit-sharing investment accounts
QIS	Quantitative Impact Study
RI	Responsible investment
ROA	Return on assets
ROE	Return on equity
RSAs	Regulatory and supervisory authorities
RSPs	Rural Support Programmes
SAG	Standards and Guiding Principles
SAMA	Saudi Arabian Monetary Agency
SBBA	Sale and Buy-Back Agreement
SBIS	Sharī`ah-based Bank Indonesia Certificate
SBP	State Bank of Pakistan
SEA	South-East Asia
SHF	Shareholders" Fund
SIFIs	Systemically important financial institutions
SKRAs	Strategic Key Result Areas

SLOLR Sharī`ah-compliant lender of last resort

SLR Statutory Liquidity Requirement

SMEs Small- and medium-sized enterprises

S&P Standard & Poor"s

SPP Strategic Performance Plan

SRI Socially responsible investment

SSS Scripless Securities Settlement

TD Top-down

UAE United Arab Emirates

UK United Kingdom

UN United Nations

UNEP FI United Nations Environment Programme Finance Initiative

UNHRC United Nations Human Rights Council

UNICEF United Nations Children's Fund

UPSIA Unrestricted profit-sharing investment accounts

US United States

References

AAOIFI. (n.d.). Governance Standard for Islamic Financial Institutions No. 7 *Corporate Social Responsibility Conduct and isclosure for Islamic Financial Institutions*: Accounting and Auditing Organization For Islamic Financial Institutions (AAOIFI).

Abdelhamid, D., & El Mahdi, A. (2003). *The small business informality challenge: lessons learned from country experiences and the road ahead of Egypt.* Paper presented at the Economic Research Forum Working Papers.

Abu-Tapanjeh, A. M. (2009). Corporate governance from the Islamic perspective: A comparative analysis with OECD principles. *Critical Perspectives on Accounting, 20*(5), 556-567. doi:10.1016/j.cpa.2007.12.004

Al-Rifaee, S. (2008). Islamic banking myths and facts.

Alasrag, H. (2010). Global Financial crisis and Islamic finance.

Ali Aribi, Z., & Gopinath Arun, T. (2012). Corporate Social Responsibility in Islamic Financial Institutions (IFI): A Management Insight. *Available at SSRN 2052635.*

Allen&OveryLLP. (2009). Islamic microfinance report for institutions offering Islamic financial services.

Ayub, M. (2009). *Understanding Islamic Finance*: Wiley.

Brown, D. (2013). *Corporate social responsibility.* (A Senior Thesis submitted in partial fulfillment of the requirements for graduation in the Honors Program), Liberty University.

Cernat, L., López , A. N., & T-Figueras, A. D. (2014). SMEs are more important than you think! Challenges and opportunities for EU exporting SMEs. Chief Economist Note, vol 3. Brussels: European Commission. Available from http://trade.ec.europa.eu/doclib/docs/2014/september/tradoc_152792.pdf.

Chapra, M. U. (2007). 21 Challenges facing the Islamic financial industry. *Handbook of Islamic Banking*, 325.

Chapra, M. U. (2011). The global financial crisis: Some suggestions for reform of the global financial architecture in the light of Islamic finance. *Thunderbird International Business Review, 53*(5), 565-579.

Chapra, M. U., & Ahmed, H. (2002). Corporate governance in Islamic financial institutions. *Occasional Paper No. 6, Jeddah, IRTI/IDB.*

Dewar, J., & Hussain, M. M. (2011). ISLAMIC PROJECT FINANCE. In J. Dewar (Ed.), *International Project Finance: Law and*

Practice: OUP Oxford.

Di Mauro, F., Caristi, P., Couderc, S., Di Maria, A., Ho, L., Grewal, B. K., . . . Zaher, S. (2013). *Islamic finance in Europe*. Retrieved from

Elasrag, H. (9. April 2011). Principals of the Islamic finance: A focus on project finance. *MPRA Paper No. 30197.*

Elasrag, H. (2010). Enhancing the competitiveness of the Arab SMEs. *Available at SSRN 1586454.*

European commission. (2015). User guide to the SME Definition. doi:10.2873/782201
10.2873/620234

Faiz, W. (2011). *Challenges and opportunities Islamic financial institutions are facing in the western countries.* (Master Thesis), University of Aarhus.

Farook , S. (2007). On corporate social responsibility of Islamic financial institutions. *Islamic Economic Studies, 15*(1), 31-46.

Friedman, M. (1962, 1982). *Capitalism and freedom.* United States of America: University of Chicago press.

Friedman, M. (September 13, 1970). The Social Responsibility of Business is to Increase its Profits. *The New York Times Magazine.*

Ghuddah, A. S. A. (1998). Ijarah (lease). *Dallah Al-Baraka Group Al-Baraka Banking Group*

(ABG) Department of Research & Development.

Haniffa, R., & Hudaib, M. (2007). Exploring the ethical identity of Islamic banks via communication in annual reports. *Journal of Business Ethics, 76*(1), 97-116.

Hasan, Z. (2009). Corporate Governance: Western and Islamic Perspectives. *International Review of Business Research Papers, 5*(1), 277-293.

Hasan, Z. (2010). Regulatory framework of Shari'ah governance system in Malaysia, GCC Countries and the UK. *Kyoto Bulletin of Islamic Area Studies, 3*(2), 82-115.

Hasan, Z. (2011). *Sharīʿah Governance in Islamic Financial Institutions in Malaysia, GCC Countries, and the UK.* (Doctoral thesis), Durham University. Retrieved from http://etheses.dur.ac.uk/810/

Hassan, A., & Latiff, S. B. A. (2009). Corporate social responsibility of Islamic financial institutions and businesses: Optimizing charity value. *Humanomics, 25*(3), 177-188.

IFC. (2014). Islamic Banking Opportunities Across Small and Medium Enterprises in MENA

Ilias, S. (2010). *Islamic finance: overview and policy concerns.* Retrieved from http://www.fas.org/sgp/crs/misc/RS22931.pdf

International Labour Office. (2015). *Small and medium-sized enterprises and decent and productive employment creation* Retrieved from Geneva, Switzerland:

International Trade Centre (ITC). (2015). *SME Competitiveness Outlook 2015: Connect, Compete and Change for Inclusive Growth.* Geneva: ITC.

Iqbal, Z. (1997). Islamic financial systems. *Finance and Development, 34*, 42-45.

Iqbal, Z. (2007). Challenges facing Islamic financial industry. *Journal of Islamic Economics, Banking and Finance (JIEBF), 3.*

Islamic Financial Services Board. (May 2015). *Islamic Financial Services Industry Stability Report 2015* Retrieved from Malaysia:

Jamali, D., & Mirshak, R. (2007). Corporate social responsibility (CSR): theory and practice in a developing country context. *Journal of business ethics, 72*(3), 243-262.

Léon, F., & Weill, L. (2016). *Islamic Banking Development and Access to Credit.* Université de Strasbourg: Laboratoire de Recherche en Gestion et Economie (LaRGE)

Maali, B., Casson, P., & Napier, C. (2006). Social reporting by Islamic banks. *Abacus, 42*(2), 266-289.

Malaysia International Islamic Financial Centre. (February 2016). *Islamic finance: Bridging the Funding Gaps of SMEs and MSMES.* Retrieved from Malaysia:

Mohammed, J. A. (2007). *Corporate social responsibility in Islam.* Auckland University of Technology.

Moon, J. (2011). Corporate Social Responsibility. *Manchester Business School.*

Muhammada, M. Z., & Chonga, R. (2007). The Contract of Bay'Al-Salam and Istisna'in Islamic Commercial Law: A comparative analysis. *Labuan e-Journal of Muamalat and Society, 1*, 21-28.

Mumani, H. F. (2014). *Islamic Finance for SMEs in Jordan 1978-2014.* (Master of Science in Banking and Finance), Eastern Mediterranean University (EMU)-Doğu Akdeniz Üniversitesi (DAÜ).

Navas-Alemán, L., & Guerrero, T. (2016). *Procurement practices and SMEs in global supply chains: what do we know so far? : A literature review*

Geneva: ILO, : International Labour Office, Enterprises Department.

OECD. (2004). *OECD Principles of Corporate Governance 2004*: OECD Publishing.

OECD. (2016). *Financing SMEs and Entrepreneurs 2016*: OECD Publishing.

Rasameel Structured Finance. (2014). *2013 Annual*

Global Sukuk Report. Retrieved from

S&P Shariah Indices Methodology, (March 2014).

Saidi, N. (2008). Corporate governance in Islamic finance. *Islamic Wealth Management: A Catalyst for Global Change and Innovation. London: Euromoney Institutional Investor.*

Shaban, M., Duygun, M., & Fry, J. (2016). SME's lending and Islamic finance. Is it a "win–win" situation? *Economic Modelling, 55*, 1-5. doi:http://dx.doi.org/10.1016/j.econmod.2016.01.029

UK Islamic finance secretariat UKIFS. (2013). *financial markets series UK*. Retrieved from

United States International Trade Commission (USITC). (2014). Trade Barriers That U.S. Small and Medium-sized Enterprises perceive as affecting exports to the European Union, Investigation No. 332-541, Publication 4455. Washington, D.C.
Available from http://www.usitc.gov/publications/332/pub4455.pdf.

Usmani, M. I. A., & Zubairi, Z. (2002). Meezan Bank's Guide to Islamic Banking: Karachi: Darul-Ishaat Urdu Bazar.

Uusmani, M. T. (2002). *An introduction to Islamic finance* (Vol. 20): Brill.

Wajdi Dusuki, A. (2008). What does Islam say about corporate social responsibility? *Review of*

Islamic Economics, 12(1), 5-28.

World Bank Group, & Islamic Development Bank. (2015). *Leveraging Islamic Finance for Small and Medium Enterprises (SMEs)*. Retrieved from Washington DC:

Zyp, V. L. (2009). *Islamic finance in the United States: Product development and regulatory adoption.* Georgetown University.

Wilson, Rodney (2009). 'Shariah Governance for Islamic Financial Institutions'. Journal of Islamic Finance 1(1): 59-75.

www.ingramcontent.com/pod-product-compliance
Lightning Source LLC
Chambersburg PA
CBHW050525240926
51846CB00003B/701
* 9 7 8 2 0 7 2 2 9 3 6 1 0 *